Josh McDowell, Ron Luce, Dave Bellis

The Revolt Workbook

Visit Tyndale's exciting Web site at www.tyndale.com

The Revolt Workbook

Cover illustration by Kevin Conrad and Jeremy Cox. Cover design by Kirk DouPonce: UDG Designworks. Cover art copyright © 2003 Tyndale House Publishers. All rights reserved.

Some portions of this book were adapted from *Beyond Belief to Convictions*. Copyright © 2002 by Josh McDowell, Bob Hostetler, and David H. Bellis. Used by permission of Tyndale House Publishers, Inc., Wheaton, Illinois 60189. All rights reserved.

The Message, Copyright © 1994 by Eugene H. Peterson. Used by permission of NavPress, P.O. Box 35001, Colorado Springs, CO 80935. All rights reserved.

Produced with the assistance of The Livingstone Corporation (www.LivingstoneCorp.com). Project staff includes Cheryl Blum, Ashley Taylor, Kirk Luttrell, and Joanna Guest.

Unless otherwise indicated, all Scripture quotations are taken from the *Holy Bible*, New Living Translation, copyright © 1996. Used by permission of Tyndale House Publishers, Inc., Wheaton, Illinois 60189. All rights reserved.

Scripture quotations marked NIV are taken from the *Holy Bible*, New International Version® NIV® Copyright © 1973, 1978, 1984 by International Bible Society. Used by permission of Zondervan Publishing House. All rights reserved.

Scripture quotations marked NASB are taken from the *New American Standard Bible*, © 1960, 1962, 1963, 1968, 1971, 1972, 1975, 1977 by the Lockman Foundation. Used by permission. All rights reserved.

Scripture quotations marked NCV are taken from the *Holy Bible, New Century Version*, © 1987, 1988, 1991 by Word Publishing. Used by permission. All rights reserved.

Printed in the United States of America

ISBN 0-8423-7978-9

1. Undated Elective Curriculum/High School 2. Undated Elective Curriculum/Junior High and Middle School

Table of Contents

Section One: A Transformed Life

Section Two: A Crucified Life

Section Three: A Separated Life

Section Four: A Mission in Life

Authors and Writer

About the Authors

AUTHORS Josh McDowell and Ron Luce collaborated with their writer to bring you this workbook based on Josh McDowell's *Beyond Belief to Convictions* book and Ron Luce's messages and ministry.

Josh McDowell is an internationally known speaker, author, and traveling representative of Campus Crusade for Christ. He has authored or coauthored more than sixty books including *More Than a Carpenter* and *The New Evidence That Demands a Verdict*. Josh and his wife, Dottie, have four children and live in Texas.

Ron Luce is founder and president of Teen Mania Ministries, which sends youth on short-term missions around the globe, hosts weekend Acquire the Fire events reaching over 150,000 teenagers annually, and offers a precollege training program called the Honor Academy. Ron is a traveling speaker, author, and host of a Christian TV program. He and his wife, Katie, have three children and live in Texas.

About the Writer

DAVE BELLIS developed the educational design of *The Revolt Workbook* course, developed the course outline, and created the activities and assignments based on Josh and Ron's material and on the input of over sixty creative young people. Dave then wrote this workbook.

Dave Bellis is a ministry consultant focusing on ministry planning and product development. He has pioneered the interactive video and workbook educational design now used by more than 100,000 churches and small groups worldwide. He is a writer, producer, and campaign coordinator for Josh McDowell's campaigns. He and his wife, Becky, have two grown children and live in northeastern Ohio.

Acknowledge-ments

Thank You!

WE WOULD LIKE to thank the many people who brought creativity and insight to creating this workbook:

Over sixty interns at the Honor Academy in Garden Valley, Texas, for their passion and creativity in brainstorming and field-testing the activities. Though I (Dave Bellis) told you that your names would appear on the acknowledgment page, complete records were not kept of all your participation, and we ran out of time tracking you down. Please accept my apology for not naming you individually. Your contribution was nonetheless invaluable. Thank you, and may God give you a special blessing since I can't list you individually here.

Bob Hostetler for collaborating with us on the direction of this workbook, editing it thoroughly, and managing the entire editorial process.

Nathaniel Dame, Ann Phillips, and Alina Ramirez for their excellent coordination of the flow of information between Teen Mania and the writers, as well as administering the brainstorming and field-testing of the material.

Judy Drewry, Casey Wolston, Jennifer Murphy, and Bethany Engelstad for expediting all the notes, dictation, and input from Ron Luce. You all are such a joy to work with.

Rod Arnold for masterfully managing all the details at Teen Mania and communicating on behalf of Ron Luce. Your passion and gentle spirit made working on this project together a delight.

Lynn Vanderzalm of Tyndale House Publishers for her guidance and wise counsel on the content and for helping us communicate each concept clearly.

Janis Whipple for her skillful editing (and doing so in record time).

Jim Baird, who, as the production manager, kept the process rolling and worked through the maze of details to bring the work to the typesetting stage.

And finally, to the campaign team at Tyndale House who so graciously endured the process with us.

Josh McDowell
Ron Luce
Dave Bellis

Ready, Set, Hold It!

Three Questions

YOU'RE ABOUT TO BEGIN a revolutionary journey. But before you start, you should answer three questions about this workbook course:

1. Who is this for?

The Revolt Workbook is for anyone who wants to know what real life—true life—is all about. It is for those who are able to see through the hype and slick sales job of a world that says real happiness revolves around your own wants and pleasures. It is for those who can stand the truth—the truth that real happiness and meaning in life aren't about seeking your own pleasure and fulfilling selfish desires. It is for those who sense that true happiness and meaning are found in feeling wanted and needed; in giving, loving, and being loved; in belonging and being accepted no matter what; in feeling connected, secure, and never being truly alone. These things define a real, satisfying relationship, and *The Revolt Workbook* is for anyone who wants that kind of relationship.

What will probably surprise you, though, is this: A real relationship—one that results in the happiness and meaning you long for—doesn't come cheap. Experiencing it will cost you something. It doesn't take much to get rejected, ridiculed, abandoned, left out, betrayed, taken advantage of, or just to feel alone. But it does cost something to live a life in which you sense your very purpose for living, in which you feel connected and secure, cherished and cared for, loved and understood. If you want that, this workbook is for you. You are about to embark on a journey to discover that the culture of the cross of Jesus Christ is the true source of your strength, happiness, and meaning in life. An intimate, never-ending connected relationship with Jesus Christ is the answer to the very meaning of life itself. We call it the CrossCulture life. And to experience it will only cost you one thing—your life!

"If any of you wants to be my follower, you must put aside your selfish ambition, shoulder your cross daily, and follow me. If you try to keep your life for yourself, you will lose it. But if you give up your life for me, you will find true life."

Jesus (Luke 9:23-24)

2. How does this work?

WHAT YOU HAVE in front of you is a self-discovery workbook. Every week following the group meeting with your youth group, you will complete five daily exercises in this workbook. The first two will take you fifteen to twenty minutes each. The last three are devotional readings.

But here's the thing: All those exercises, readings, and questions will lead you to discover a new characteristic of the CrossCulture life (there are four characteristics). You will also be asked to complete assignments. They won't be easy because each one in some way requires that you give up some part of your life. But we're not the ones asking you to do that—Jesus Christ himself is—and we think you'll find it's worth it.

Another thing. There is an online dimension to this workbook. Your youth leader probably gave you an access code to the MyCrossCulture.com/prayer site. That code allows you to complete your day 1 exercise of each week on a special Web site designed just for you. You'll also find daily devotions there, and will be able to post your prayer requests and interact with your youth group via that online connection. If your youth leader didn't give you the access code numbers, call him or her and ask about it. All the details are in his or her *The Revolt Leader's Guide*.

3. Where is this going?

THIS WORKBOOK is only the beginning. It outlines what the CrossCulture life is about. Other material will follow. The bottom line is this: This workbook course opens up a journey with Christ that will not only revolutionize your life but also the world around you. And you are an important part of that revolution. In fact, by becoming a passionate follower of Christ, you are becoming part of what may well become your very own CrossCulture Revolution!

SECTION ONE
A Transformed Life

Transformed

Transformed
Transformed
Transformed
Transformed
Transformed
Transformed
Transformed
Transformed
Transformed
Transformed
Transformed
Transformed
Transformed
Transformed
Transformed
Transformed
Transformed
Transformed
Transformed
Transformed
Transformed
Transformed
Transformed
Transformed

Transformed

Who Were We Meant to Be?

WELCOME to the first group session in *The Revolt!* These next seven weeks will be a life-changing, world-changing experience. So . . . let's get started!

The following pages are intended for use in the group session; you'll be instructed by your leader when and how to complete them.

Whaddya Know?

LIST BELOW three things you didn't previously know about someone in your youth group:

1. _____

2. _____

3. _____

Deepest Desires / Greatest Fears

LIST BELOW what you think are most peoples' three deepest desires:

1. _____

2. _____

3. _____

LIST BELOW what you think are most peoples' three greatest fears:

1. _____

2. _____

3. _____

Week One
Group Session 1
Week One
Group Session 1
Week One
Group Session 1
Week One
Group Session 1
Week One
Group Session 1
Week One
Group Session 1
Week One
Group Session 1
Week One
Group Session 1
Week One
Group Session 1
Week One
Group Session 1
Week One
Group Session 1
Week One
Group Session 1
Week One
Group Session 1
Week One

Making the Connection

FIRST, trade workbooks with your partner.

Below are questions to use as you interview your partner (your partner will also interview you); record your partner's responses below (you'll return the workbook to him or her and receive your own back at the end of this activity).

LIST some of the places you usually look for happiness and meaning:

_____

_____

_____

_____

_____

_____

_____

_____

_____

To most of us, it *FEELS* so natural and right to believe that we have what it takes to find happiness and meaning on our own, from within ourselves . . . or at least from other people (friends, boyfriends, girlfriends). Does that describe how you feel most of the time? (circle one)

YES   NO

READ ALOUD the words of Jesus (below):

> *"I am the true vine, and my Father is the gardener. He cuts off every branch that doesn't produce fruit, and he prunes the branches that do bear fruit so they will produce even more. You have already been pruned for greater fruitfulness by the message I have given you. Remain in me, and I will remain in you. For a branch cannot produce fruit if it is severed from the vine, and you cannot be fruitful apart from me."*

"Yes, I am the vine; you are the branches. Those who remain in me, and I in them, will produce much fruit. For apart from me you can do nothing. Anyone who parts from me is thrown away like a useless branch and withers. Such branches are gathered into a pile to be burned. But if you stay joined to me and my words remain in you, you may ask any request you like, and it will be granted!" (John 15:1-7)

WHAT DO YOU THINK Jesus meant when he said, "Apart from me you can do nothing?" Did he mean you can't get out of bed in the morning? Pour a bowl of cereal? Get your driver's license? Discuss with your partner what you think he meant, and write a summary on the lines below:

_____

_____

_____

_____

_____

NOW, EXCHANGE WORKBOOKS AGAIN, and continue this activity in your own workbook. Look at the Bible verses below. A word has been left out of each verse. Choose from the word list and see if you can fill in the correct word in each of the verses:

Word List:
me, myself, I, we, ourselves, us, them, friends, family, Christ, relationships

● *It's in _____ that we find out who we are and what we are living for. (Ephesians 1:11, The Message)*

● *"_____ satisfies every need there is." (Acts 17:25)*

● *Everything got started in _____ and finds its purpose in him. (Colossians 1:16, The Message)*

Is the meaning of Jesus' words in John 15:1-7 becoming any clearer?

You see, if a lamp isn't plugged into a power source, it won't light. If the branch of a vine isn't attached to the stem, it won't grow.

Week One
Group Session 1
Week One
Group Session 1
Week One
Group Session 1
Week One
Group Session 1
Week One
Group Session 1
Week One
Group Session 1
Week One
Group Session 1
Week One
Group Session 1
Week One
Group Session 1
Week One
Group Session 1
Week One
Group Session 1
Week One
Group Session 1
Week One
Group Session 1

The one who designed us did so in order that we would produce fruit and enjoy the happiness and meaning we long for, only by being connected to the source of all good things (see James 1:17).

So . . . all the strength, abilities, and potential we may have won't result in happiness and meaning . . . apart from God. Though we may not be used to seeing it that way, and though it may not always seem that way, we'll discover just how true it is as we go further in our workbooks and group sessions together.

(When you finish the above exercise, close your workbooks to let your group leader know you're done.)

God's Jealousy Is Good

Week 1 | Day 1

Life without a Mechanical Power Source

IMAGINE waking up this morning to find that the power source to all mechanical energy was gone. There was no longer any electrical power. Water and wind generators were gone. Gasoline, oil, coal, natural gas, or energizing batteries could no longer power anything mechanical.

Imagine your life with:

- No electrical lights
- No furnace or air conditioning
- No refrigeration
- No computers, e-mail, or Internet
- No radios or CDs
- No PalmPilots or calculators
- No cars, trucks, trains, and planes

- No washing machines
- No TV
- No telephone
- No hairdryers, curling irons, or electric razors
- No indoor plumbing

This means the modern lifestyle, as you know it, would come to a sudden halt.

- Think of what life would be like at your house.
- How would your school function differently?
- Think of what would happen to medical science.
- Imagine the change it would bring to factories and offices.
- Consider how your eating habits would change.

Civilization would return to a primitive culture. Many who depended upon mechanical machinery and devices for jobs would be out of work. Chaos, famine, and many deaths would no doubt follow. Life without the power source for mechanical energy would be devastating to the inhabitants of this earth. But as bad as that would be, what would living without the relational power source be like?

Life without the Relational Power Source

You probably know that the happiness and meaning you want out of life is found in relationships—feeling accepted, secure, respected, valued, and appreciated; being understood, being wanted, belonging, and so on.

But imagine living in a world totally separated from the one power source of all that relational happiness and meaning—God. To even begin to grasp this, we must be reminded that relational happiness and meaning exist apart from you and me.

READ the following verses:

▶ *Whatever is good and perfect comes to us from God above. (James 1:17)*

▶ *It's in Christ that we find out who we are and what we are living for. (Ephesians 1:11, The Message)*

▶ *He [Christ] gives life and breath to everything, and he satisfies every need there is. (Acts 17:25)*

▶ *"Apart from me you can do nothing." (John 15:5)*

NOW, MARK AN ANSWER below to indicate whether you agree or disagree.

1. Life and all that makes it good can exist without God. With God life is simply better.

2. While it may seem like we can live apart from Christ, the fact is, remove his Spirit's presence and power from the world and we would be void of life and all its meaning.

3. God made us dependent upon him because he wants us to always be connected relationally to him.

4. Those religions that don't believe Christ is the absolute provider of all relational happiness and meaning can still find satisfaction and fulfillment in life because there is no one way that is true for everyone.

Did you disagree with numbers 1 and 4 and agree with numbers 2 and 3? When you accept that God is *the* relational power source of all life, it means you are totally dependent on him to experience the relational happiness and meaning he has in store for you.

If God was totally removed from us, add to the list what "life" would consist of.

- Darkness
- Aloneness
- Helplessness
- _____
- _____
- _____
- _____

Someone has said that death without God is complete separation from him . . . which defines what hell actually is: absolute aloneness in an existence void of life and goodness from God.

I ◯ agree ◯ disagree that life without the relational power source of God is infinitely worse than living without a mechanical power source.

Why God Is a Jealous God

The reality of God being a jealous God is directly related to his desires and efforts to keep us relationally connected to him. The very first of the Ten Commandments God gave us was "Do not worship any other gods before me" (Exodus 20:3). God went on to say he is "a jealous God who will not share your affection with any other god!" (Exodus 20:5). But why? Why did God not want us to worship any other gods? Why must he have our focused love?

NOTE: Go now to www.MyCrossCulture.com/prayer to complete this lesson.

If your group leader has signed you up for your CrossCulture e-prayer group, go there to complete the rest of this lesson online. You will need to follow the instructions and register. You can access daily devotionals, send and receive prayer requests within your group, and exchange messages among your group. It is your own private CrossCulture group, exclusively for you. Details of this free service and how to access it are found in the group leader's guide. Ask your youth worker how to take advantage of your own CrossCulture e-prayer group.

Week One
Day 1
Week One
Day 1
Week One
Day 1
Week One
Day 1
Week One
Day 1
Week One
Day 1
Week One
Day 1
Week One
Day 1
Week One
Day 1
Week One
Day 1
Week One
Day 1
Week One
Day 1
Week One
Day 1
Week One
Day 1

CROSSCULTURE™

"You must worship no other gods, but only the Lord, for he is a God who is passionate about his relationship with you." (Exodus 34:14)

You don't have to be the brightest bulb in the box to spot what some people see as your highest purpose in life. Your math teacher thinks you're just a slice of brain desperate to pass algebra. Your soccer coach assumes your one mission in life is to practice, practice, and practice some more until you can make enemy goalies cry. And your after-school boss has you scheduled to flip burgers on the graveyard shift for the next fifty years. But God made you for far more. He is a jealous God who does not want to share your focused love with any other. He designed you to love him and be loved by him completely. He made you to know him and be known intimately by him. He longs to bring you into a mind-blowing relationship with him so you can be whom he meant you to be (his child) and live as you were meant to live (an adventurous, exciting life of fulfillment and meaning that honors and pleases him).

So why do you think God is jealous of his relationship with you?

_____

_____

_____

_____

READ THIS:

"And now, Israel, what does the Lord your God require of you? He requires you to fear him, to live according to his will, to love and worship him with all your heart and soul, and to obey the Lord's commands and laws that I am giving you today for your own good." (Deuteronomy 10:12)

God is a jealous God because . . .

Check those you think apply:

- ○ Loving him protects you.
- ○ He just doesn't like competition.
- ○ He has your best interest at heart.
- ○ He is your only true source of relational happiness and meaning in life.
- ○ He knows serving him is what is best for you.
- ○ He is an angry God.
- ○ He wants to take the fun out of life.

Is God really jealous because he knows that without him you can never be truly happy or fulfill your meaning in life? Is it really true that "apart from me [Christ] you can do nothing" (John 15:5)? How does it make you feel that God is so passionate about his relationship with you that he wants you exclusively for himself?

_____

_____

_____

_____

_____

My Assignment: Create My Prayer

God knows that loving and worshiping him with all your heart and soul is in your best interest. Yet that kind of committed and exclusive relationship isn't always easy to maintain. Some things tend to hinder you from always keeping your relationship with God first priority. Check (✓) which things you think apply to you. Then add to the list below other things that hinder you from keeping God a priority in your life.

○ Not enough praying that focuses on my relationship with God.
○ Failing to know God better through my Bible reading.
○ Allowing other relationships to come between God and me.

● _____

● _____

● _____

● _____

● _____

● _____

● _____

● _____

Week One
Day 1
Week One
Day 1
Week One
Day 1
Week One
Day 1
Week One
Day 1
Week One
Day 1
Week One
Day 1
Week One
Day 1
Week One
Day 1
Week One
Day 1
Week One
Day 1
Week One
Day 1
Week One

19

Create a prayer to God that asks him to help you deal with your hindrances so you can focus more on him being your priority relationship.

Here is an example. Dear God, I pray that you will help me this week to make you a higher priority in my life by:

1) Taking time alone with you in prayer.
2) Reading your love letter to me—your Holy Word.
3) Honoring my parents by . . .
4) Refusing to go . . .
5) Refusing to watch . . .
6) Refusing to talk critically about . . .

NOW PREPARE your own prayer to God.

Dear God, I pray that you will help me this week to make you a higher priority in my life by:

_____

_____

_____

_____

_____

_____

_____

_____

Now that you have created your prayer, take the step of asking your friends in your youth group to pray for you. Post your prayer request on the e-prayer site and request that your group pray that you will make Christ a higher priority in your life. Invite them to send their prayer requests to you. The CrossCulture is a praying culture.

The earnest prayer of a righteous person has great power and wonderful results. (James 5:16)

You Were Meant to Keep Only What You Give Away

The Sea That Died

THERE ARE TWO SEAS in the land of Israel.

One is a scene of beauty, a center of commerce whose shores and depths teem with life. Fish abound in its waters. Carpeted slopes of rich grass encircle this sea. The surrounding countryside is a patchwork of noisy villages and valued farmland.

The other sea boasts none of those characteristics. Its shores are barren, the atmosphere is harsh, and its bitter waters cannot sustain life or quench thirst.

The difference is in the giving.

The Dead Sea receives fresh water daily from the Jordan River, but keeps it. All the minerals halt their flow within its boundaries.

The Sea of Galilee, however, sparkles with freshness because it not only receives the water that flows down from the northern mountains but also gives itself to the winding Jordan River as it flows to the south.

The only sea that remains alive is the one that allows water to flow through it. The only way it stays fresh is by giving its freshness away.

You and I are no different. You can only keep what you give to others. Wise King Solomon said, "It is possible to give freely and become more wealthy, but those who are stingy will lose everything. The generous prosper and are satisfied; those who refresh others will themselves be refreshed" (Proverbs 11:24-25).

You Can't Give What You Don't Have

"IT'S A GIMMICK!" skeptical Stan says. "People want us to be generous and give to others, so they tell us we can only keep what we give away. But the truth is if people give too much of themselves, they will be drained emotionally. We've got to be careful not to give too much to others or we won't have enough for ourselves."

Does Stan have a point? Let's do the math. For example, Stan has one hundred gallons of comforting care. And Stan's friend Chad needs sixty gallons of that comfort because he just suffered a breakup with his girlfriend. How much comforting care would Stan have left?

Stan's	100	gallons of comforting care
Chad's	− 60	gallons for breakup

_____ gallons of remaining comforting care

Everything is fine so far. But what happens if Sarah, Stan's other friend, isn't chosen to be a cheerleader? She's really bummed out that she's been rejected. She needs fifty gallons of comforting care. How much will Stan have left?

Stan's	100	gallons of comforting care
Chad's	− 60	gallons for breakup
Sarah's	− 50	gallons for rejection

_____ gallons of remaining comforting care

Stan's conclusion: He doesn't have enough comforting care to go around. He must be careful how much he gives to others or he won't have enough for himself.

It All Depends on Your Source

Do you agree with Stan's conclusion? If all you have is a limited source of comforting care, you will soon run dry. It's true, you can't give what you don't have. But remember, the Sea of Galilee gives and keeps on giving because it receives from the unlimited source of the Jordan River.

It is impossible to meet the comforting needs of all your friends if you are your own source of comforting care. Your success in prospering spiritually and emotionally is based upon which resource you draw your power from.

READ THIS:

All praise to the God and Father of our Lord Jesus Christ. He is the source of every mercy and the God who comforts us. He comforts us in all our troubles so that we can comfort others. When others are troubled, we will be able to give them the same comfort God has given us. (2 Corinthians 1:3-4)

1. What is one reason God comforts you?

_____

_____

2. Whose comfort do you give out? _____

3. How much comfort does God have to flow through you?

_____

_____

      Because God has an endless supply of love, comforting care, support, acceptance, etc., you need never run out—no matter how much you give. Like a mighty river flowing in and through a lake, you can remain full while you give and keep on giving to others when you receive from the unlimited resource of God.

> *Dear friends, let us continue to love one another, for love comes from God. . . . This is real love. It is not that we loved God, but that he loved us and sent his Son as a sacrifice to take away our sins.*
>
> *Dear friends, since God loved us that much, we surely ought to love each other. No one has ever seen God. But if we love each other, God lives in us, and his love has been brought to full expression through us. (1 John 4:7, 10–12)*

Fill in the blanks based upon the above Scripture passage.

1. Love comes from _____ .

2. This is real _____ .

3. If we love each other, God lives in _____ and his love has

been brought to full expression _____ us.

My Assignment:
Flowing God's Love through Me to Another

READ MATTHEW 22:37-39 IN YOUR BIBLE.

Who did Jesus say we must love?

1. _____

2. _____

Week One
Day 2
Week One
Day 2
Week One
Day 2
Week One
Day 2
Week One
Day 2
Week One
Day 2
Week One
Day 2
Week One
Day 2
Week One
Day 2
Week One
Day 2
Week One
Day 2
Week One
Day 2
Week One

How did he say we are to love them?

1. With _____

_____

2. As _____

Identify one expression of love toward God that you desire to show him this week.

_____

_____

_____

Now identify an expression of God's love through you to another. For example, express God's comforting care to someone who is hurting, lift someone's load through a supportive act, share a thoughtful word to someone who needs encouragement, or visit a sick person. Commit some random act of God's love, and let his unlimited power source of love flow through you.

Be prepared to overflow with what you give away. This is what you were meant to be and do—be a CrossCulture child of God in which he flows his love to you and then through you.

From God's unlimited relational power source I plan to express his love to:

_____   (someone's name)   by

_____

_____

May you experience the love of Christ, though it is so great you will never fully understand it. Then you will be filled with the fullness of life and power that comes from God. (Ephesians 3:19)

**Access your daily devotionals at MyCrossCulture.com/prayer. If you are not using the e-prayer group, you will be given daily devotional readings here in this workbook to be read over the next three days.

Daily Devotional

Week 1 | Day 3

Read Jeremiah 2:11—13

Why is it so difficult to admit that God is the source of all my strength?

_____

_____

_____

_____

Week 1 | Day 4

Read Ephesians 1:9—11

Why do you think God chose you? How does it make you feel that he has? Tell him how you feel.

_____

_____

_____

_____

Week 1 | Day 5

Read 1 John 4:16—19

Can you really love like God without experiencing his love firsthand? Why or why not?

_____

_____

_____

_____

Week One
Days 3–5
Week One
Days 3–5
Week One
Days 3–5
Week One
Days 3–5
Week One
Days 3–5
Week One
Days 3–5
Week One
Days 3–5
Week One
Days 3–5
Week One
Days 3–5
Week One
Days 3–5
Week One
Days 3–5
Week One
Days 3–5

Week Two
Group Session 2
Week Two
Group Session 2
Week Two
Group Session 2
Week Two
Group Session 2
Week Two
Group Session 2
Week Two
Group Session 2
Week Two
Group Session 2
Week Two
Group Session 2
Week Two
Group Session 2
Week Two
Group Session 2
Week Two
Group Session 2
Week Two
Group Session 2
Week Two
Group Session 2
Week Two

It Takes a Miracle to Be Who You Were Meant to Be

Week 2 Group Session 2

THE BIBLE describes the condition of every one of us—whether we realize it or not—ever since we were born into this sinful world. Colossians 2:13 says,

> *You were dead because of your sins and because your sinful nature was not yet cut away. Then God made you alive with Christ. He forgave all our sins. (Colossians 2:13)*

But that's not all. It goes on to say:

> *He canceled the record that contained the charges against us. He took it and destroyed it by nailing it to Christ's cross. (Colossians 2:14).*

If you're prepared to commit—or recommit—to a transformed life in Christ, pray:

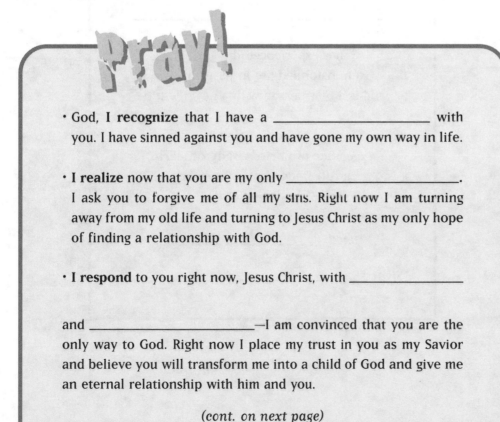

Pray!

• God, **I recognize** that I have a _____ with you. I have sinned against you and have gone my own way in life.

• **I realize** now that you are my only _____.
I ask you to forgive me of all my sins. Right now I am turning away from my old life and turning to Jesus Christ as my only hope of finding a relationship with God.

• **I respond** to you right now, Jesus Christ, with _____

and _____—I am convinced that you are the only way to God. Right now I place my trust in you as my Savior and believe you will transform me into a child of God and give me an eternal relationship with him and you.

(cont. on next page)

27

- **I rely** upon you to _____ my life from death to life. You said in John 11:25 that I will be given eternal life by believing in you and that I will never perish. I am believing and relying on you to transform me into your child right now.

- Thank you for doing what you said you would do. Thank you for making me a forgiven child of God and bringing me into a relationship with the one true God. Please live the transformed life of Christ in and through me every day. I pray these things in Jesus' name, amen.

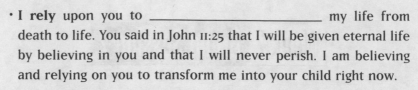

My New I.D.

This certifies that

_____

has experienced the gift of
a transformed life in Jesus Christ,
and is a new person with a new identity:

**a child of God,
a member of Christ's body on earth,
a full-fledged revolutionary
of the CrossCulture**

Dated _____

Signed _____

The Magical Grape

It may sound incredible, but there is a magical species of grape found not far from where you live. Eating this grape will give you astonishing energy—so much energy, in fact, that you won't need to eat or drink another thing for a year. And you can have this grape simply for the asking.

Now, you're probably thinking this is a joke, right? But what if I told you it's really true—well, sort of. That is, the magic is really going to come from within you, because if you believe—truly believe—that the grape has this amazing property, it *will*. So your job is to believe in the magic of the grape. *Really* believe, hard and long. And your believing will make the grape magical.

Are you buying all this? Why not? Probably because you don't accept the claim that any amount of believing is going to make a grape magical, right? But think about that for a moment. If you're saying my claim about the grape isn't true, then the grape's power isn't real, either. And no amount of believing in the grape is going to make it work. Do you agree?

If something isn't true, believing in it isn't going to make it real. Right?

Believe it (or not)!

Do You Believe These Things Are True?

Check (✓) the answer to indicate whether you believe it is true or false.

1. Sin brings death—separation from God. "When people sin, they earn what sin pays—death" (Romans 6:23, NCV).

2. Without a relationship with God, we have no hope of true happiness in this life and no hope of eternal life. "You were dead, doomed forever because of your many sins" (Ephesians 2:1).

3. God sent Christ to die for us that we could have a relationship with God. "For God so loved the world that he gave his only Son, so that everyone who believes in him will not perish but have eternal life" (John 3:16).

4. Christ is God's perfect sacrifice for sin, and if we believe in Jesus, God will forgive us of our sins, and we can have a real relationship with God. "Then God made you alive with Christ. He forgave all our sins. He canceled the record that contained the charges against us. He took it and destroyed it by nailing it to Christ's cross" (Colossians 2:13-14).

5. Becoming a Christian is a miracle of being transformed from death to new life in Christ.

"What this means is that those who become Christians become new persons. They are not the same anymore, for the old life is gone. A new life has begun!" (2 Corinthians 5:17).

Does Believing Make It True?

DO YOU AGREE with all five statements? Then you believe sin separates us from God and we are doomed, but Christ died for us. And because of Christ and the cross, our sins can be forgiven. So when we become Christians we are raised to a new life in Christ.

It's great if you believe all that. But what if it isn't really true? What if Jesus was just a delusional man who claimed to be God's Son? What if he was a fraud? What if he never really performed miracles, and didn't actually rise from the dead? If he wasn't God's Son, the perfect sacrifice for your sins as he claimed, then how could you really be forgiven? How could your relationship with God be real?

That is a scary thought, isn't it? But the truth is, your prayers to God and beliefs in Christ aren't worth anything if the claims of Christ aren't actually true. If he isn't literally the true Son of the living God, then nothing of the relationship you think you have with God is real. If your faith is placed in a Christ who isn't whom he claimed to be, then all of your believing is as worthless as believing in a magical grape.

"Wait a minute," you protest. "Doesn't my own experience of feeling forgiven by God count for anything?"

No one is trying to deny your relationship with God here, or cause you to doubt it. But that relationship is based not on what you feel is real, but on what is actually true about Christ. If he isn't whom he said he was, then he can't be what he said he'd be for you.

But here's the great news: the reverse is also true. If we can actually establish that Christ is whom he claimed to be—the one and only, true Son of God—then we can know beyond a shadow of a doubt that your relationship with God is a total reality.

NOTE: If you are signed up for the CrossCulture e-prayer group, go online now at www.MyCrossCulture.com/prayer and complete the rest of this lesson. You can post your prayer requests, receive your friends' prayer requests, interact with your youth group, and get your daily devotionals. If you are not using this online service, continue on in this workbook.

Week Two
Day 1
Week Two
Day 1
Week Two
Day 1
Week Two
Day 1
Week Two
Day 1
Week Two
Day 1
Week Two
Day 1
Week Two
Day 1
Week Two
Day 1
Week Two
Day 1
Week Two
Day 1
Week Two
Day 1
Week Two
Day 1
Week Two

Believing with Conviction

DOES IT somewhat trouble you to think that your beliefs in Christ aren't worth anything if the claims of Christ aren't actually true? Why?

_____

_____

_____

_____

Exercising faith is important, but it should not be a blind faith. The faith Jesus calls for is not a blind faith but an informed, intelligent faith—one that is supported by evidence.

John the Baptist was thrown into prison while Jesus was still alive. He obviously began to question his faith in Jesus as the true Messiah, because he sent his friends to ask Jesus, "Are you really the Messiah we've been waiting for, or should we keep looking for someone else?" (Matthew 11:3).

READ VERSES 4-5 OF MATTHEW 11.

How did Jesus respond?

_____

_____

_____

_____

Jesus clearly reminded John of the evidence that he was truly the Son of God. It was the evidence of Christ's miraculous powers of God that reinforced John's faith. But seeing the evidences doesn't eliminate the need for faith. No amount of evidence can create a 100 percent certainty. Believing something without evidence is like taking a leap into the dark; faith that is rooted in the truth is like stepping into the light. Noted author and apologist J. P. Moreland defines faith as "a trust in what we have reason to believe is true."[1] Beliefs that are rooted in the truth, supported by evidences, are beliefs with convictions.

Having _convictions_ can be defined as _being so thoroughly convinced that Christ and his Word are both objectively true and relationally meaningful that you act upon your beliefs regardless of the consequences._

[1] J. P. Moreland, _Love Your God with All Your Mind_ (Colorado Springs: NavPress, 1997), 25.

List three people you personally know or someone from history who had those kinds of convictions.

1. _____

2. _____

3. _____

The apostle Paul had those kinds of convictions. He was beaten for his faith in Christ; he was stoned and left for dead; he was imprisoned and eventually beheaded. But what did he say? "I am not ashamed; for I know whom I have believed and I am convinced that He is able to guard what I have entrusted to Him until that day" (2 Timothy 1:12, NASB). He knew the person he believed in and was so convinced in his mind and persuaded in his heart that he remained faithful to his belief, even to the point of death.

That's the kind of belief several students at Columbine High School had when guns were pointed at their heads and they were asked, "Do you believe in God?" And it cost them their lives.

The morning of April 20, 1999, sixteen-year-old Cassie Bernall, a student at Columbine, handed her friend Amanda Meyer a note that read: "Honestly, I totally want to live my life completely for God. It's hard and scary, but totally worth it!"[2] Later that day she was shot to death.

Rachel Scott was another Columbine student. One year earlier she had written in her diary "I'm not going to apologize for speaking the name of Jesus. . . I'm not going to hide the light God has put in me. If I have to sacrifice everything, I will."[3] And she did. She was also among those killed

This kind of convinced, committed belief in God and his Word is what you are challenged to pursue. You need more than personal opinions or lightly held suspicions about God and his Word; you need convictions. In the days ahead, you are undoubtedly going to risk rejection from others; you may face persecution, or even worse. As part of the CrossCulture, you need to be sure, convinced beyond a reasonable doubt that you are committing your life to something genuine, something true, something real.

In your next session (day 2) of this workbook you will discover overwhelming evidence that Christ is who he claimed to be . . . and that what he offers you is real!

My Assignment: Create My Prayer

It is as if right now Jesus is saying to you:

I want you to be convinced that I am exactly who I say I am—that
I am the Christ, the Son of the living God, and your only way to

[2] Wendy Murray Zoba, *Day of Reckoning: Columbine and the Search for the American Soul* (Grand Rapids: Baker, 2000), 85.
[3] Ibid., 180.

Week Two
Day 1
Week Two
Day 1
Week Two
Day 1
Week Two
Day 1
Week Two
Day 1
Week Two
Day 1
Week Two
Day 1
Week Two
Day 1
Week Two
Day 1
Week Two
Day 1
Week Two
Day 1
Week Two
Day 1
Week Two

have a relationship with my Father. He and I are your only true source of life, happiness, and meaning. I want you not only to believe that I speak the truth; I want you to have a conviction that I am the truth. When you are equipped with such a conviction, you will be so convinced that I am the one true God that you will believe what I say and obey those words. Not because you fear me, but because you know I am the God who "is passionate about my relationship with you." That is what convictions do; they give you the will to act upon your belief—I will do the rest.

Let Christ know that you want that kind of relationship—one that believes in him so deeply that you will follow him no matter what. Create your prayer:

Dear God, I want

_____

_____

_____

_____

_____

_____

_____

_____

Now let your CrossCulture youth group know what your prayer to God is and ask them to pray that you will develop deep convictions—convictions that will hold you steady no matter what happens in life.

Don't retaliate when people say unkind things about you. Instead, pay them back with a blessing. That is what God wants you to do, and he will bless you for it. . . . Now, who will want to harm you if you are eager to do good? But even if you suffer for doing what is right, God will reward you for it. So don't be afraid and don't worry. Instead, you must worship Christ as Lord of your life. And if you are asked about your Christian hope, always be ready to explain it. (1 Peter 3:9, 13-15)

The Proof Is in the Truth

JESUS SAID, "I am the way, the truth, and the life. No one can come to the Father except through me. If you had known who I am, then you would have known who my Father is. From now on you know him and have seen him! . . . Anyone who has seen me has seen the Father!" (John 14:6-9).

If what Jesus said is true, he would have to be God in human form. And he would have to be God to deliver on his promise to transform you from death to life. If Jesus Christ wasn't deity—the Son of the living God—then no matter how much you believed he has forgiven you or how much you think has been done in your life, it can't be real. Because Christ would have no more power than any other inspirational leader throughout history.

Let's say an aging and retired weight lifter made an extraordinary claim that he once lifted a two-thousand-pound weight over his head. How could you possibly be convinced that his claim is true? Check (✓) those that apply.

- ◯ Ask him to take a lie detector test.
- ◯ Make him cross his heart and hope to die.
- ◯ Find written newspaper or trade articles that support his claim.
- ◯ Have him swear on a stack of Bibles that it's true.
- ◯ Interview people who actually saw him lift two thousand pounds.
- ◯ Flip a coin: Heads, I believe him.

The way to be convinced this retired weight lifter, or anyone else's, claims are true is to examine the credible evidence. The statement by the person making the claim isn't sufficient evidence, because he may be lying or he may be deluded enough to believe his lie is the truth. To be convinced of the truth of what a person says requires examining evidence that can verify the Truth.

Why is it important to examine the evidence that Jesus is the Son of the one true God?

_____

_____

_____

_____

Won't Christ be a little put off by us putting him to the test? Why or why not?

_____

_____

_____

_____

There is a reason Christ has provided us with overwhelming evidence that his claims about himself are true. Notice how he appealed to his disciples: "Don't you believe that I am in the Father and the Father is in me? . . . Or at least believe *because of what you have seen me do*" (John 14:10-11, emphasis added). Christ wants us to believe with conviction. He wants us to be convinced in every fiber of our being that he is the *One* who can save us, the *One* deserving of our exclusive love and devotion.

So when Jesus walked on water (Mark 6), made the blind see (Mark 10), caused the dumb to speak (Matthew 10), raised people from the dead (Luke 7 and John 11), and a dozen other miracles, he wasn't just meeting the needs of people. He was offering evidence so that you and I would believe in him with deep conviction.

When Thomas, Jesus' disciple, heard that Jesus rose from the grave, he didn't believe it. Read John 20:24-29.

What evidence did Thomas want?

_____

_____

_____

_____

What did he say when he saw the evidence?

_____

_____

_____

_____

What did Jesus say in verse 29?

_____

_____

_____

Now notice verses 30 and 31. It says, "Jesus' disciples saw him do many other miraculous signs besides the ones recorded in this book. But these are written so that you may believe that Jesus is the Messiah, the Son of God, and that by believing in him you will have life."

You have not literally seen Christ with your own eyes and believed, like Thomas. But you can see the evidence. That is why Christ has provided his miracles, "so that you may believe . . . and that by believing him you will have life."

Name and Address Please

THE MIRACLES Christ performed are only one form of evidence that Christ was God in human form. The fulfillment of messianic prophecies—the predictions the Jewish prophets made about how the Messiah would come and what he would be like—is another.

More than four hundred years before Christ was born, God directed his prophets to foretell a lot of specific things about the Messiah. It was like identifying someone by giving his or her specific name and address. If the information was specific enough, no doubt the person in question would be found. For example, you are one person among some six billion people on this planet. If I had the task of identifying you out of the total earth's population, I could do so by learning the answers to eight questions:

    1. What continent do you live on? _____
       (Africa? Europe? North America? etc.)

Week Two
Day 2
Week Two
Day 2
Week Two
Day 2
Week Two
Day 2
Week Two
Day 2
Week Two
Day 2
Week Two
Day 2
Week Two
Day 2
Week Two
Day 2
Week Two
Day 2
Week Two
Day 2
Week Two
Day 2
Week Two

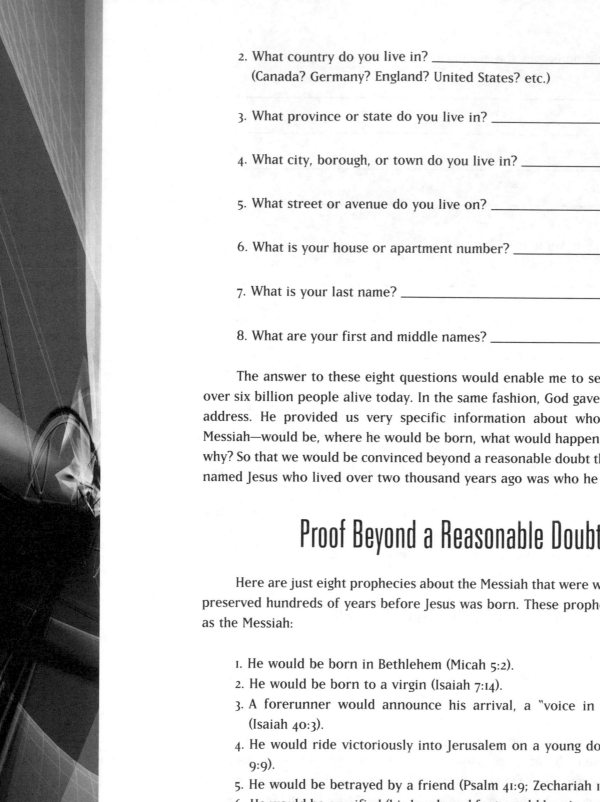

2. What country do you live in? _____
   (Canada? Germany? England? United States? etc.)

3. What province or state do you live in? _____

4. What city, borough, or town do you live in? _____

5. What street or avenue do you live on? _____

6. What is your house or apartment number? _____

7. What is your last name? _____

8. What are your first and middle names? _____

The answer to these eight questions would enable me to separate you from over six billion people alive today. In the same fashion, God gave us Jesus Christ's address. He provided us very specific information about who the Christ—the Messiah—would be, where he would be born, what would happen to him, etc. And why? So that we would be convinced beyond a reasonable doubt that a Jewish man named Jesus who lived over two thousand years ago was who he claimed to be.

Proof Beyond a Reasonable Doubt

Here are just eight prophecies about the Messiah that were written down and preserved hundreds of years before Jesus was born. These prophecies stated that as the Messiah:

1. He would be born in Bethlehem (Micah 5:2).
2. He would be born to a virgin (Isaiah 7:14).
3. A forerunner would announce his arrival, a "voice in the wilderness" (Isaiah 40:3).
4. He would ride victoriously into Jerusalem on a young donkey (Zechariah 9:9).
5. He would be betrayed by a friend (Psalm 41:9; Zechariah 11:12).
6. He would be crucified (his hands and feet would be pierced), but his bones left unbroken (Psalms 22:16; 34:20).
7. He would die (be "cut off") 483 years after the declaration to rebuild the temple in 444 B.C. (Daniel 9:24).
8. He would rise from the dead (Psalm 16:10).

Every one of these prophecies was fulfilled in Jesus' life, death, and resurrection. But couldn't that all be a coincidence? Perhaps those prophecies have been fulfilled in any number of people. Right?

This is where the science of statistics and probabilities comes in. Professor Peter W. Stoner, in an analysis that was carefully reviewed and pronounced to be sound by the American Scientific Affiliation, states that the probability of just *eight* of those prophecies being fulfilled in one person is 1 in 10^{17} (that's 1 in 100,000,000,000,000,000).

Look at it this way: if you were to take 100,000,000,000,000,000 silver dollars and spread them across the state of Texas, they would not only cover the entire state, they would form a pile of coins two feet deep! Now, take one more silver dollar, mark it with a big red X, toss it into that pile, and stir the whole pile thoroughly.

Then, blindfold yourself, and starting at El Paso on the western border of the state, walk the length and breadth of that enormous state, from Amarillo in the panhandle to Laredo on the Rio Grande all the way to Galveston on the Gulf of Mexico, stooping just once along the way to pick up a single silver dollar out of that two-foot-deep pile . . . then take off your blindfold and look at the silver dollar in your hand. What are the chances that you would pick the marked coin out of a pile of silver dollars the size of the Lone Star State? *The same chance that one person could have fulfilled just eight messianic prophecies in one lifetime.*

And that's just the beginning! More than three hundred messianic prophecies in the Old Testament were fulfilled in *one person,* Jesus Christ—and all of them were made over four hundred years prior to his birth. In other words, it is nearly unthinkable to imagine that the Old Testament prophecies about the Messiah could have come true in one man unless, of course, he is—as he himself claimed—"the Messiah, the Son of the Blessed God" (Mark 14:61), the One who was and is and is to come (see Revelation 4:8).

My Assignment: Survey My Christian Friends

You can know—be totally convinced—that whatever Christ promises he can deliver. Why? Because he is God. The transformation you have experienced in Christ is real because everything Jesus Christ claimed about himself is true—objectively true. Christ *is* the Son of the living God. It is not true because you believe it. You believe it because it is true. That means you can be confident, no matter how you may feel from day to day, that your trust in Christ and his promises is secure.

Your Assignment: This week tell three Christian friends (not part of your youth group) that you are doing an unscientific survey. Then ask them, "Is Christ the Son of God because you believe it or do you believe it because it is true?" Then share with them what you have been learning this week from these lessons.

Jesus made some extraordinary promises to you that could only be made and delivered on if he were God. He said:

> *"I am the resurrection and the life. Those who believe in me, even though they die like everyone else, will live again. They are given eternal life for believing in me and will never perish. Do you believe this?" (John 11:25-26)*

Week Two
Day 2
Week Two
Day 2
Week Two
Day 2
Week Two
Day 2
Week Two
Day 2
Week Two
Day 2
Week Two
Day 2
Week Two
Day 2
Week Two
Day 2
Week Two
Day 2
Week Two
Day 2
Week Two
Day 2
Week Two
Day 2
Week Two

Do you *really* believe this? Why?

_____

_____

_____

_____

Thank Christ for being who he is and giving you a new life—one that will live forever.

**Access your daily devotionals at MyCrossCulture.com/prayer or come back here each day for your devotional reading assignment.

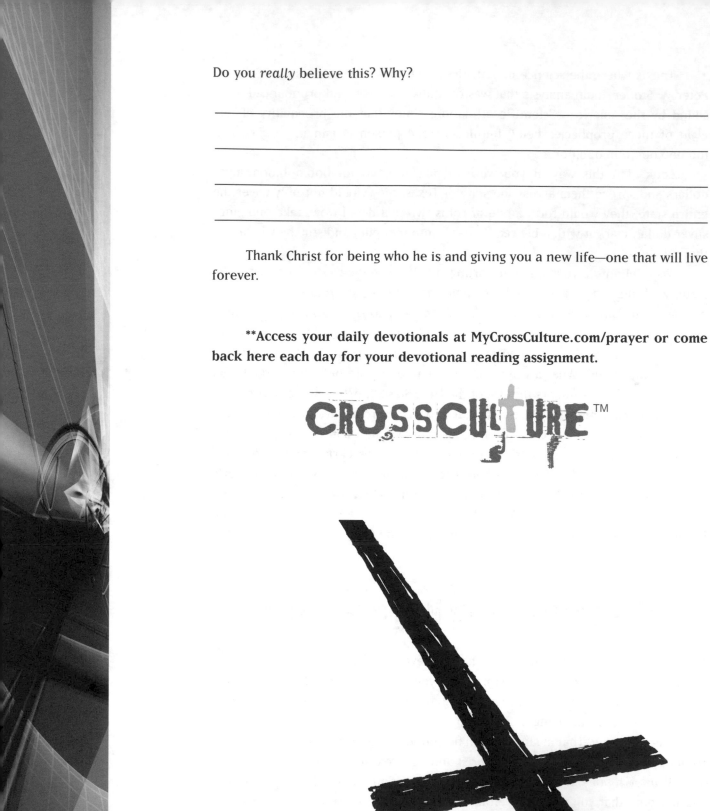

Daily Devotional

Week Two
Days 3-5
Week Two
Days 3-5
Week Two
Days 3-5
Week Two
Days 3-5
Week Two
Days 3-5
Week Two
Days 3-5
Week Two
Days 3-5
Week Two
Days 3-5
Week Two
Days 3-5
Week Two
Days 3-5
Week Two
Days 3-5
Week Two
Days 3-5
Week Two
Days 3-5
Week Two

Week 2 Day 3

Read Colossians 2:13—14

How extensively have the sin charges against you been destroyed? Can they ever resurface to be used against you? Why or why not?

_____

_____

_____

_____

Week 2 Day 4

Read Micah 7:18—19

Do you find it hard to grasp that God can't remember your sins? How does that make you feel?

_____

_____

_____

_____

Week 2 Day 5

Read John 1:10—13

Since you are a child of God, what family characteristics do you have? Identify an attitude or action that you now have that is like your heavenly Father.

_____

_____

_____

_____

41

SECTION TWO
A Crucified Life

Crucified

Crucified
Crucified
Crucified
Crucified
Crucified
Crucified
Crucified
Crucified
Crucified
Crucified
Crucified
Crucified
Crucified
Crucified
Crucified
Crucified
Crucified
Crucified
Crucified
Crucified
Crucified
Crucified
Crucified
Crucified
Crucified
Crucified

Crucified

The CrossCulture Life:
A Spirit of Self-Sacrifice

HEBREWS 12:1 SAYS:

> *Let us strip off every weight that slows us down, especially the sin that so easily hinders our progress. And let us run with endurance the race that God has set before us. (Hebrews 12:1)*

And Jesus said,

> *"If any of you wants to be my follower, you must put aside your selfish ambition, shoulder your cross daily, and follow me." (Luke 9:23)*

Even though we are transformed into new life with Christ, and our sin record is nailed to Christ's cross when we come to him in repentant faith, we are still hindered by our selfish desires . . . these must be crucified, nailed to the cross as well.

GALATIANS 5:24 SAYS:

_____

_____

_____

_____

_____

_____

_____

THOUGHT QUESTIONS:

1. "I know Paul says I should nail my selfish desires to the cross. But I

_____

_____

_____

_____ ."

2. "I know my selfish desires don't get me what I want; instead, they lead to

_____

_____

_____

_____ ."

3. "But sometimes I don't deny my selfish desires because

_____

_____

_____

_____ ."

4. "And sometimes I don't feed my godly desires because

_____

_____

_____

_____ ."

5. "If I don't crucify my selfish desires, I'll probably

_____

_____

_____

_____ ."

6. "If I do crucify my selfish desires, I'll probably

_____

_____

_____

_____ ."

Week Three
Group Session 3
Week Three
Group Session 3
Week Three
Group Session 3
Week Three
Group Session 3
Week Three
Group Session 3
Week Three
Group Session 3
Week Three
Group Session 3
Week Three
Group Session 3
Week Three
Group Session 3
Week Three
Group Session 3
Week Three
Group Session 3
Week Three
Group Session 3

A Problem Well-Defined is Half Solved

Seeing the Real Problem

SHERYL LOVED FIXING UP THINGS. She loved spending her summer breaks helping her dad renovate old homes, which they would then resell or rent to others. To her it was like a "makeover" on a grand scale. She thought it was so exciting to walk through an old house discussing with her dad what they would do to make it better. Sometimes they would make major changes, like knocking down walls or tearing up old floors. Other times they would totally transform the appearance of a house with a fresh paint job and a few new electrical fixtures. She loved it all—the destruction and the construction, the heavy work and the touch-up jobs.

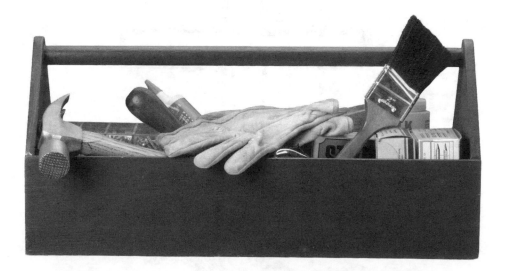

But one house became a nightmare. Two weeks after replastering the walls and applying a beautiful paint job, her father noticed a crack in the new plaster. Sheryl patched up the crack and applied new paint. A month later, as they walked through the renovated house with prospective tenants, the people pointed out cracks in the plaster—the same cracks Sheryl had fixed before. She was so frustrated! She told the would-be renters that she was sure she had corrected the imperfection, yet it seemed her efforts had not solved the root problem.

After the prospective tenants left, Sheryl and her father conducted a thorough examination in the basement of the house. That's when they discovered a sizeable crack in the foundation. The real problem, they learned, was not a plaster problem at all, but a foundation problem. They could repair the plaster a hundred times and it wouldn't solve anything, because the real problem was an uneven foundation.

Once they learned the real cause, the problem was half solved.

The Blame Game

THE CROSSCULTURE LIFE is fulfilling because "he has called us to receive his own glory and goodness! And by that same mighty power, he has given us all of his rich and wonderful promises" (2 Peter 1:3-4).

The reason many people struggle in their Christian life and don't experience God's glory and goodness, riches and promises, is that they fail to define the root problem that hinders them. Instead of getting to the root of the problem, they engage in a defensive "Blame Game."

READ GENESIS 3:8-13.

What was Adam's answer to God when asked if he had eaten the forbidden fruit?

_____

_____

_____

What was Eve's response when God asked her what she had done?

_____

_____

_____

How do you tend to respond when you are accused of something? Why?

_____

_____

_____

Week Three
Day 1
Week Three
Day 1
Week Three
Day 1
Week Three
Day 1
Week Three
Day 1
Week Three
Day 1
Week Three
Day 1
Week Three
Day 1
Week Three
Day 1
Week Three
Day 1
Week Three
Day 1
Week Three
Day 1
Week Three
Day 1
Week Three

Self—Good or Bad?

WE ARE ALL PLAGUED with a nature that doesn't want to accept blame, be at fault, or suffer a wrong. Some call this our selfish nature, the sinful nature, the flesh, the old self. The Bible says, "You laid aside the old self with its evil practices, and have put on the new self" (Colossians 3:9-10, NASB).

Yet the Bible also says, "For you have been called to live in freedom—not freedom to satisfy your sinful nature, but freedom to serve one another in love. For the whole law can be summed up in this one command: 'Love your neighbor as yourself'" (Galatians 5:13-14).

Indicate which statements you believe are true or false.

1. I get hungry every day. I do eat, but it is selfish and wrong of me.

True   False

2. At times in my life I have felt disrespected by someone. It is selfish and wrong of me to want respect.

True   False

3. I want to get good grades at school. It is selfish and wrong of me to cheat to get those good grades.

True   False

4. I don't like being rejected by people. It is selfish and wrong of me to hate them for it.

True   False

5. I want my parents and peers to be proud of me. It is selfish and wrong of me to do things to get their approval.

True   False

There is a difference between self-love and selfishness. Obviously we are to love ourselves, otherwise we wouldn't know how to love our neighbors. Yet there is a selfish sin nature that seeks to fulfill only its own desires. This self-centered, selfish nature needs to be crucified. "Those who belong to Christ Jesus have nailed the passions and desires of their sinful nature to his cross and crucified them there" (Galatians 5:24).

[NOTE: If you are signed up and part of the CrossCulture e-prayer group, please go online to complete the rest of this lesson. You can also access your daily devotionals there, send and receive prayer requests, and exchange messages within your youth group.]

**Continue on with this workbook lesson if you do not wish to use the Cross-Culture site.

Identify the Nature that Lurks Within

WHEN YOUR SINS were nailed to Christ's cross, God transformed you from death to life. His life gave you *real* life—a life in relationship with him. It was that experience that made you God's child. You and I are to live out that new life experience every day. But there is something within you that will hinder your new Father/child relationship—unless it is dealt with. Paul the apostle explains it this way:

> *Since you have been raised to new life with Christ, set your sights on the realities of heaven. . . . Let heaven fill your thoughts. Do not think only about things down here on earth. For you died when Christ died, and your real life is hidden with Christ in God. And when Christ, who is your real life is revealed to the whole world, you will share in all his glory.*
>
> *So put to death the sinful, earthly things lurking within you.* (Colossians 3:1-5)

Specifically what are the sinful, earthly things that are lurking within you? These are the appetites and desires that are not honoring to God. These are the attitudes and actions that are not pleasing to God. Be honest and transparent with God right now and identify what lurks within you that needs put to death. What do these things look like and sound like in your life? No one will be reading what you write here. Go to Galatians 5:19-21 and Colossians 3:5-9 in your Bible and read how Scripture identifies what the sinful nature does.

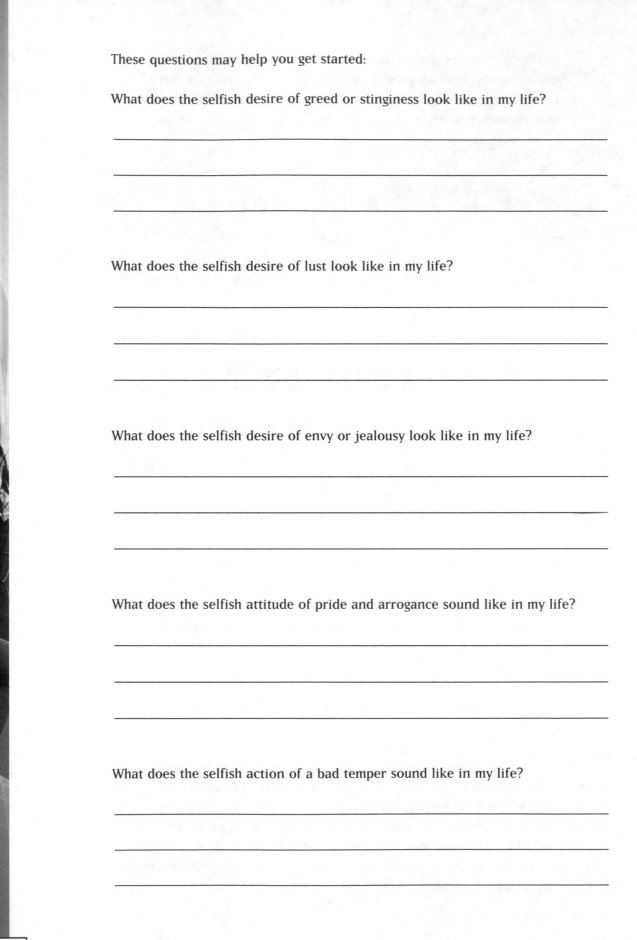

These questions may help you get started:

What does the selfish desire of greed or stinginess look like in my life?

_____

_____

_____

What does the selfish desire of lust look like in my life?

_____

_____

_____

What does the selfish desire of envy or jealousy look like in my life?

_____

_____

_____

What does the selfish attitude of pride and arrogance sound like in my life?

_____

_____

_____

What does the selfish action of a bad temper sound like in my life?

_____

_____

_____

Other desires, appetites, attitudes, and actions that represent the sinful nature in me are:

_____

_____

_____

_____

_____

_____

What Do I Do with What I Find?

If you are like most of us, what you find lurking within isn't pretty. But by defining the problem within, you have the problem half solved. The very fact that you have identified certain desires, attitudes, and actions that are not honoring to God pinpoints those areas that need to be put to death. And the first step in that death process is confession.

> *If we confess our sins to him, he is faithful and just to forgive us and to cleanse us from every wrong. . . .*
>
> *My dear children, I am writing this to you so that you will not sin. But if you do sin, there is someone to plead for you before the Father. He is Jesus Christ, the one who pleases God completely. (1 John 1:9; 2:1).*

My Assignment: Create My Prayer

Jesus is your advocate—the one who pleads your case before the Father. Create your prayer to God. Tell him of the selfish desires, attitudes, and actions that you have pinpointed in your life. Tell him you want those "sinful, earthly things lurking within you" to be put to death. Tell him you intend to renounce those appetites each day for the next month, refusing to give into them, and daily surrendering instead to his Spirit's control in those areas.

Week Three
Day 1
Week Three
Day 1
Week Three
Day 1
Week Three
Day 1
Week Three
Day 1
Week Three
Day 1
Week Three
Day 1
Week Three
Day 1
Week Three
Day 1
Week Three
Day 1
Week Three
Day 1
Week Three
Day 1
Week Three
Day 1
Week Three
Day 1
Week Three

Dear God,

_____

_____

_____

_____

_____

_____

_____

Now that you have created your prayer, you can ask your friends in your group to pray for you by posting your prayer at www.MyCrossCulture.com/prayer in your own online prayer journal, which you can make accessible to others in your group. You may or may not want to modify your prayer before you post it. It's okay to be vulnerable with those who are good friends, those with whom you can have confidence that your prayer requests are safe (of course, it is always safe to trust your deepest thoughts and feelings to God).

Let your group know that as part of the CrossCulture, you intend to continually have your selfish desires nailed to Christ's cross.

> *You have died with Christ, and he has set you free from the evil powers of this world. (Colossians 2:20)*

Winning!

YOU'RE UP EARLY to run. You exercise. You practice. You eat right. It isn't easy. In fact, it's downright painful: You deny yourself certain foods; you stretch and punish your muscles; you grunt and groan as you work out, until your lungs gasp for air and your face drips with sweat.

But you do it. You deny yourself and endure the pain because, if you've heard your coach bellow it once, you've heard it a thousand times: "No pain, no gain."

You do it because you believe your coach is right. All the painful exercising and practice pays off when the game or competition ends or you cross the finish line . . . as a winner. The roar of the crowd, the cheers of the fans, the high-fives of your teammates, and all the jubilation of victory says "Well done!" Real satisfaction, the thrill of gratification, comes when you give up comfort and ease in order to win the prize. There is real gain from the pain.

In Death There Is Life——Real Life

Having your selfish nature put to death is painful. It's not easy to turn your back on pleasures and appetites of the flesh. The CrossCulture life *does* include self-sacrifice. But what kind of sacrifice is it?

READ ROMANS 12:1.

What does it mean to give our bodies to God?

_____

_____

_____

We are to die, yet we are to live. And in giving up our lives, we gain.

> *"If any of you wants to be my follower, you must put aside your selfish ambition, shoulder your cross daily, and follow me. If you try to keep your life for yourself, you will lose it. But if you give up your life for me, you will find true life." (Luke 9:23-24)*

If we are to be followers of Christ we must:

1. _____

2. _____

3. _____

"And if you give up _____

you will _____."

    Someone might say: "I don't want to be ungrateful or anything, but in all this death to self and sacrificing myself and giving up my life, don't I lose my own identity? Christ may offer the 'true life,' but do I lose all traces of me? Is it wrong to want Christ to save me without me having to lose the real me?"

    READ GALATIANS 2:17-21. In this passage Paul is dealing with the distinctions of the law of God and our faith in Christ. Then Paul says he's been crucified with Christ.

Do I lose my personhood when I give up my life for Christ? Who do I think is living, then—Christ? Me? Or both?

_____

_____

_____

_____

_____

_____

    Paul uses the personal pronouns "I," "my," "me," or "myself" eighteen times in three verses as he explains that he is crucified with Christ. Apparently the real you still exists when you are crucified with Christ.

Our old life—that self-centered nature that wants what it wants when it wants it—must be put to death.

Read Galatians 5:22-25. Then see if you can draw a line from left to right, connecting each of the old-life characteristics with the nine transformed characteristics of a new life in Christ. (The first one has been done as an example.)

THE OLD LIFE . . .	TRANSFORMED INTO . . .	. . . THE NEW LIFE
Evil & self-centered		Love
Rude & impatient		Joy
Insensitive & harsh		Peace
Hateful & ungiving		Patience
Despondent & sad		Kindness
Discontented & dissatisfied		Goodness
Undisciplined & unruly		Faithfulness
Mean & uncaring		Gentleness
Disloyal & undependable		Self-control

The Real Gain——Is the Real You with a New Nature

Crucifying the old nature may be painful because it is giving up what your selfish nature craves. But living out the desires of the sinful nature is not truly fulfilling and satisfying, nor is it how you were meant to live. The real you—the person you were meant to be—is a liberated you, free of the enslaving appetites of the sinful nature.

Paul referred to these enslaving appetites when he said, "Oh, what a miserable person I am! Who will free me from this life that is dominated by sin? Thank God! The answer is in Jesus Christ our Lord" (Romans 7:24-25).

57

The real you was meant to have a nature like God's Son, Jesus (see Romans 8:29). "God created people in his own image; God patterned them after himself; male and female he created them" (Genesis 1:27). While sin destroyed that image and likeness, Christ is in your life to restore it. By crucifying the old nature and living out your new nature, you are completed and given the relational happiness and meaning you were destined to experience.

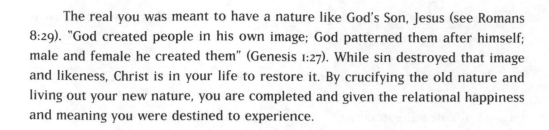

My Assignment:
Display My New Nature to Others

Colossians 3 is all about putting the old nature to death and living out the new nature. It talks about how your new nature is continually being renewed:

> *You have clothed yourselves with a brand-new nature that is continually being renewed as you learn more and more about Christ, who created this new nature within you. (Colossians 3:10)*

The real you is being continually renewed and conformed to Christ's image. What does that really look like? Colossians 3:12-17 reveals at least ten reflections or qualities of the real you. Read these verses and identify those qualities, then indicate how much you sense you need that in your life. (The first new nature quality is identified here as an example. Fill in your name and then complete the rest of the exercises.)

Since God chose _____ (your name) to be the holy [person] whom he loves, [I] must clothe [myself] with . . . (v. 12) what? What new nature qualities do I need?

1a. I need the quality of _____*tenderhearted mercy*_____ (from v. 12 of NLT).

1b. I need that   ○ very little   ○ some   ○ quite a bit   ○ a whole lot.

2a. I need the quality of _____ (from v. 12).

2b. I need that   ○ very little   ○ some   ○ quite a bit   ○ a whole lot.

3a. I need the quality of _____ (from v. 12).

3b. I need that   ○ very little   ○ some   ○ quite a bit   ○ a whole lot.

4a. I need the quality of _____ (from v. 12).

4b. I need that   ○ very little   ○ some   ○ quite a bit   ○ a whole lot.

5a. I need the quality of _____ (from v. 12).

5b. I need that   ○ very little   ○ some   ○ quite a bit   ○ a whole lot.

6a. I need the quality of _____ (from v. 13).

6b. I need that   ○ very little   ○ some   ○ quite a bit   ○ a whole lot.

7a. I need the quality of _____ (from v. 14).

7b. I need that   ○ very little   ○ some   ○ quite a bit   ○ a whole lot.

8a. I need the quality of _____ (from v. 15).

8b. I need that   ○ very little   ○ some   ○ quite a bit   ○ a whole lot.

9a. I need the quality of _____ (from v. 15).

9b. I need that   ○ very little   ○ some   ○ quite a bit   ○ a whole lot.

10a. I need the quality of _____ (from v. 16).

10b. I need that   ○ very little   ○ some   ○ quite a bit   ○ a whole lot.

Your assignment: Seek this week to display the clothes of your new nature. Any one quality will do, but be intentional about it. Begin your quiet time each day by asking God to increase the evidence of that quality in your thoughts and actions that day. Consciously seize every opportunity to be kind—or humble, gentle, forgiving, etc.—to someone this week. Pray that God will empower you with the new nature—your real life—so that it reflects on and glorifies the Lord Jesus.

> *And whatever you do or say, let it be as a representative of the Lord Jesus, all the while giving thanks through him to God the Father. (Colossians 3:17)*

Week Three
Day 2
Week Three
Day 2
Week Three
Day 2
Week Three
Day 2
Week Three
Day 2
Week Three
Day 2
Week Three
Day 2
Week Three
Day 2
Week Three
Day 2
Week Three
Day 2
Week Three
Day 2
Week Three
Day 2
Week Three
Day 2
Week Three

Be sure to make note of the "gain" you receive from displaying your new nature. Come back to this page of your workbook and indicate:

I sensed or felt _____

when I reflected honorably upon Christ by what I did or said.

**Access your daily devotional at MyCrossCulture.com/prayer or come back to your workbook each day for our devotional assignment.

Daily Devotional

Week Three
Days 3–5
Week Three
Days 3–5
Week Three
Days 3–5
Week Three
Days 3–5
Week Three
Days 3–5
Week Three
Days 3–5
Week Three
Days 3–5
Week Three
Days 3–5
Week Three
Days 3–5
Week Three
Days 3–5
Week Three
Days 3–5
Week Three
Days 3–5
Week Three
Days 3–5
Week Three

Week 3 Day 3

Read Romans 8:10–11

List three or four words or phrases that describe how you feel about a God who has gone to such lengths to have you live with him forever.

_____

_____

_____

_____

Week 3 Day 4

Read Micah 7:18–19

Does it amaze you that the most powerful and absolutely perfect being of the universe said he came to serve rather than to be served? Why?

_____

_____

_____

_____

Week 3 Day 5

Read Galatians 2:19–21

Christ lives in you. How can you make him more at home in your heart today?

_____

_____

_____

_____

The CrossCulture Life: A Spirit of Commitment

WHETHER WE REALIZE IT or not, each of us whose life has been transformed by Jesus Christ has two forces in our lives that are in conflict with the other:

- the self, that sinful part of us which wants to please only ourselves, and
- the Holy Spirit, who wants to please Christ.

The Bible says, in Galatians 5:17 (fill in the blanks):

The old sinful nature loves to _____ __ _____,

which is just opposite from what _____ _____

_____ wants. And the _____ gives us

desires that are _____ from what the _____

_____ desires. These two forces are constantly fighting

each other, and your choices are never free from this conflict.

It also says, in 2 Corinthians 5:15:

He died for everyone so that those who receive his new life will no

longer live to _____

_____. Instead, they will live to _____

_____, who died and was raised for them.

Use the lines below to journal a prayer (or prayers), asking for the Holy Spirit to increase your desire to please Christ instead of yourself:

_____

_____

_____

_____

_____

_____

_____

_____

_____

_____

_____

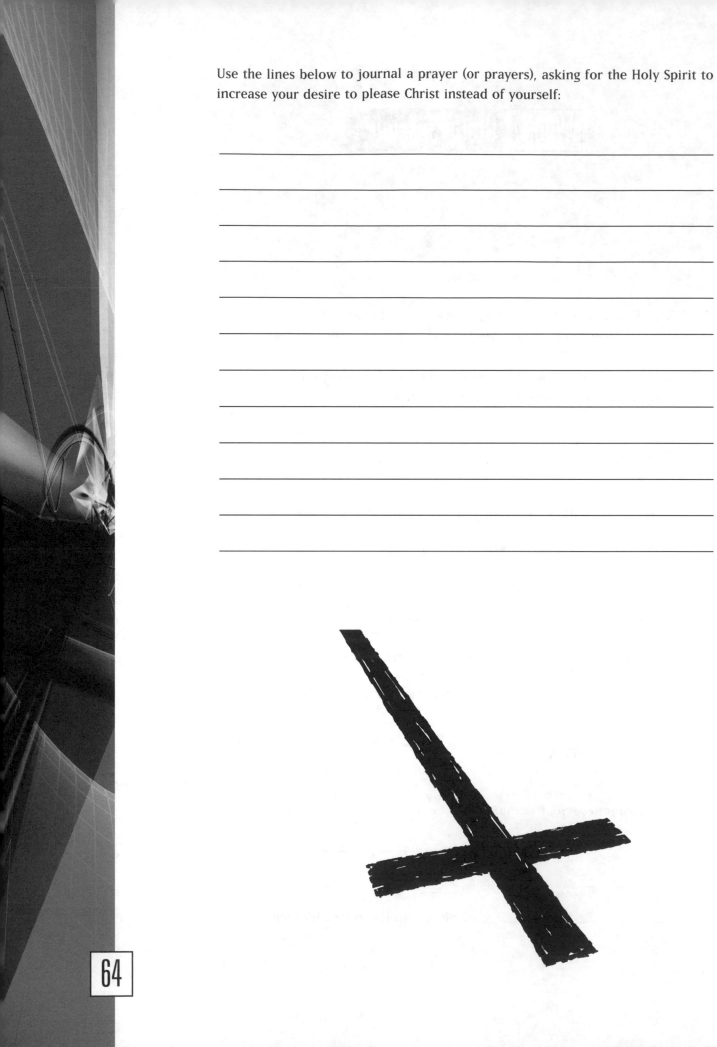

What Is Your Commitment Based Upon?

I Do?

"OH, ISN'T SHE a beautiful bride," remarked the lady with the huge hat in the fourth row as she watched Marci glide down the aisle of the church.

"And I can't imagine how much that dress cost," her friend replied.

Mark, the groom, stood tall but sweated profusely as he watched his soon-to-be wife come ever closer.

"Dearly beloved," the minister bellowed out. "We are gathered here in the presence of God to lock this man and this woman into Holy Bondage—a binding, all-encompassing commitment that will forever tie these two people together until they die."

Marci swallowed hard. Mark wiped more sweat from his brow.

"Do you, Mark Michael," the minister bellowed, pointing his bony finger at him, "promise this woman, Marci Marie, to always stay committed to her no matter what?"

Mark forced a smile and began to speak when the minister lunged toward the couple. "I mean really committed!" he roared. "Will you work day and night to support her, not complain if she can't cook like your mom or won't lift her finger to clean the house or if she stops fixing herself up to look pretty? So will ya? Now answer! Will ya?"

"I guess I will," Mark said softly.

"Guess?!" the minister snapped. "What do you mean, 'Guess?' You've got to sign a contract here in front of all these witnesses that says you'll work at your commitment, in sickness and health, like it or not, day and night, and never let up. That's what the institution of Holy Bondage is all about."

"It is?" Marci whispered, casting a confused look at her groom.

"You bet your bridal bouquet it is," the minister intoned.

65

Commitment to What?

You've probably never been to a wedding quite like that. At least, we hope not. But that's how some people view the whole subject of commitment.

Make no mistake. The CrossCulture life definitely involves a spirit of commitment, but it is not a spirit of bondage. Not at all. The spirit of commitment we're talking about and learning about is not a spirit of gloomy, grit-your-teeth-and-gut-it-out obedience merely for the sake of obedience itself.

READ THIS CAREFULLY:

> *"Hear, O Israel! The Lord is our God, the Lord is one! You shall love the Lord your God with all your heart and with all your soul and with all your might. These words, which I am commanding you today, shall be on your heart." (Deuteronomy 6:4-6, NASB)*

What is God commanding Israel to do?

_____

_____

_____

Where do those verses say the words, the commandments of God, are to be?

_____

_____

_____

What exactly do you believe you're supposed to be committed to?

_____

_____

_____

Our relationship with God is similar to the marriage commitment between a man and a woman. Marriage is not a set of promises based solely on commitment. Rather, it's about a man and woman committing themselves and pledging themselves to each other because of the love they share. Their commitment to be faithful and true is a result of their love.

A Matter of Context

You may have heard it said: Rules *without* a relationship lead to rebellion, and rules *with* a relationship lead to response. The formula looks like this:

RULES — RELATIONSHIP = REBELLION
RULES + RELATIONSHIP = RESPONSE

Nothing is wrong with committing ourselves to follow the commandments of God, his rules for righteous behavior. Certainly, we must make a commitment to do what is right.

But when our commitment is a commitment to a "what" (the rules) rather than a "whom" (God himself), we can end up feeling like poor Mark or Marci. Not only that, but also that kind of commitment can easily lead to legalism.

LOOK UP JOHN 14:23 and fill in the blanks below. Jesus said,

"All those who _____ _____ will do what I say."

You see, our commitment is first and foremost to a person, not to precepts. Our commitment must arise out of our love for God and our desire to please him. We are to obey not because we live in fear but because we truly want to please the one we love.

What motivates you to do good? A fear of the consequences? Or a loving smile from the one you love?

_____

_____

_____

Fear-based commitment is bondage and sorrow. Love-based commitment is freeing and gratifying.

> [NOTE: If you are signed up and part of the CrossCulture e-prayer group, please go online to complete the rest of this lesson. You can, of course, access your daily devotionals, send and receive prayer requests, and interact with your group.]

CROSSCULTURE™

**Continue on with this workbook lesson if you do not wish to use the Cross-Culture site.

Week Four
Day 1
Week Four
Day 1
Week Four
Day 1
Week Four
Day 1
Week Four
Day 1
Week Four
Day 1
Week Four
Day 1
Week Four
Day 1
Week Four
Day 1
Week Four
Day 1
Week Four
Day 1
Week Four
Day 1
Week Four
Day 1
Week Four
Day 1
Week Four
Day 1
Week Four

A Love That Motivates a Commitment

Read the story of the wayward son in Luke 15:11-24. Indicate whether these statements are true or false.

1. The prodigal son considered himself worthy to be taken back by his father.

2. The son asked for a loan from his father upon returning home.

3. Before the son could even get to his father's house, the father ran out to embrace him.

4. The father asked his son to pay back all that he squandered, plus 12 percent interest.

5. There is no record that the father even scolded the wayward son who came home.

God is love, and all who live in love live in God, and God lives in them. . . . Such love has no fear because perfect love expels all fear. (1 John 4:16, 18)

Fear can be the basis for certain behavior, even good behavior. But fear is never the basis for a good relationship. Yet we sometimes obey out of fear.

Have you ever found yourself obeying God out of a fear? Why or why not?

_____

_____

_____

_____

What is it about a person's relationship with God that tends to cause him to see God as an authoritarian parent who demands obedience?

_____

_____

_____

_____

_____

My Assignment: Create My Prayer

GOD IS the most loving Father you could ever imagine. The CrossCulture life is one that commits to pleasing him not out of fear but rather out of love. "So you should not be like cowering, fearful slaves. You should behave instead like God's very own children, adopted into his family—calling him 'Father, dear Father.' For his Holy Spirit speaks to us deep in our hearts and tells us that we are God's children" (Romans 8:15-16).

Share openly with God how you might not always view him as a loving, compassionate Father who has your best interest at heart. Let him know you want to see him that way and obey him always out of a heart of love, not out of a heart of fear.

Dear Father,

_____

_____

_____

_____

_____

_____

_____

Week Four
Day 1
Week Four
Day 1
Week Four
Day 1
Week Four
Day 1
Week Four
Day 1
Week Four
Day 1
Week Four
Day 1
Week Four
Day 1
Week Four
Day 1
Week Four
Day 1
Week Four
Day 1
Week Four
Day 1
Week Four
Day 1
Week Four

Let your group know your prayer request by posting your prayer. Pray for your friends who have posted their requests and let them know you are praying for them.

So now there is no condemnation for those who belong to Christ Jesus. For the power of the life-giving Spirit has freed you. (Romans 8:1-2)

In the Beginning . . .

THINK ABOUT the first human, Adam, who walked this planet in the Garden of Eden. In the beginning, everything was perfect: a paradise of grasses and flowers, and animals of all kinds under a canopy of clouds and sky that must have painted a breathtaking canvas of perfection and beauty.

Each new morning brought with it a certain combination of forms, colors, textures, sounds, and movements that converged to bring pleasure to Adam's senses. Musical birds and sparkling waterfalls filled the air. Lush tropical trees and plants grew delicious fruit, whose taste and textures spelled joy to the palate and satisfaction to the body. As this first human watched the sun go down each day, he must have gazed in awe as the multicolored clouds lit up the horizon.

The world was his very own gallery painted in such beautiful colors and depths and feelings that it captivated his soul with pure inspiration. In harmony with his environment, each enchanted evening must have brought such a satisfaction and contentment that he thought nothing could ever surpass it. Until God created woman.

Think of what might have transpired when Adam first saw the woman called Eve. Imagine how Adam might have gazed through softly waving palms to see a face so captivating that he thought he'd be content never to look at anything else again. How raptly he watched her glide toward him with elegance and grace. Her softly sculptured shape and form was like nothing he had seen before. How fast his heart beat—her beauty, her fragrance, her presence filling his senses and taking his breath away. He reached for her, in awe of this creature called woman, for in all the splendor of the Garden, he had never experienced such beauty.

But there was more to his intrigue than her glorious form. There was a mystery to this attraction. He sensed an indefinable hunger to know more than what he could physically hold and caress and enjoy . . . and so did she. They were both drawn to a deeper intimacy than their sight and touch and physical senses could experience. Planted deep within their human spirits was a desire to experientially know something about the other that they couldn't see with their human eyes or touch with their physical bodies.

What was it within the first couple that attracted them to each other? What is it within you that longs for another? Complete the sentences below.

It is a longing of the human spirit to _____

_____

_____

It is a thirst of the human heart to _____

_____

_____

It is a deep passion of the soul for _____

_____

_____

You may have listed a number of things that we long for, thirst after, and have a passionate desire for. But when you boil them all down, don't we all simply have a longing to connect, a thirst to bond, and a passionate desire to relate to another? It seems as though we are created with half a heart, and we are searching for one or more relationships to complete us. It is as if every fiber in our being craves a connectedness and oneness with others.

Why We Long for God

NOTICE how David expressed himself in the Psalms:

> *O God, you are my God; I earnestly search for you. My soul thirsts for you; my whole body longs for you in this parched and weary land where there is no water. (Psalm 63:1)*

> *As the deer pants for streams of water, so I long for you, O God. I thirst for God, the living God. When can I come and stand before him? (Psalm 42:1-2)*

Now read John 17:20-22.

What did Jesus pray that we would be? _____

_____

_____

What are we to be perfected in? _____

_____

_____

What do you think hinders you most from being one with Christ and the Father?

_____

_____

Indicate whether you agree or disagree with these statements.

1. God created me originally to be one with him, but that longing and thirst for him doesn't come naturally or automatically.

Agree   Disagree   Not Sure

2. If I practice hard at sports, it will increase my thirst for God.

Agree   Disagree   Not Sure

3. If I don't have a deep, passionate longing for God, it means I'm lost forever and have no hope of ever truly knowing God.

Agree   Disagree   Not Sure

4. If I have a greater longing for God, it seems to help me live a better Christian life.

Agree   Disagree   Not Sure

Week Four
Day 2
Week Four
Day 2
Week Four
Day 2
Week Four
Day 2
Week Four
Day 2
Week Four
Day 2
Week Four
Day 2
Week Four
Day 2
Week Four
Day 2
Week Four
Day 2
Week Four
Day 2
Week Four
Day 2
Week Four
Day 2
Week Four

How would a greater thirst and deeper longing for God help you in your Christian life?

_____

_____

_____

_____

_____

_____

It appears we long for God because he has made us to need him. Through him we find completeness and meaning in life. Yet sin has corrupted our appetites and desires. "The old sinful nature loves to do evil, which is just opposite from what the Holy Spirit wants" (Galatians 5:17). The more we refuse to feed the old nature and instead cultivate the appetites of our new nature, the more our longing and thirst for God will develop. There are ways to increase our hunger for God.

Cultivating Your Thirst

King David was a man after God's own heart who cultivated his thirst for God.

Read this passage carefully.

> I have seen you in your sanctuary
> and gazed upon your power and glory.
> Your unfailing love is better to me than life itself;
> how I praise you!
> I will honor you as long as I live,
> lifting up my hands to you in prayer.
> You satisfy me more than the richest of foods.
> I will praise you with songs of joy.
> I lie awake thinking of you,
> meditating on you through the night.
> I think how much you have helped me;
> I sing for joy in the shadow of your protecting wings.
> I follow close behind you;
> your strong right hand holds me securely. (Psalm 63:2-8)

David writes in verse 1 that his soul thirsts for God and his whole body longs for him. Then he identifies at least seven things he does—or disciplines he undertakes—that cultivate his thirst for God. List them below (the first one is completed for you):

1. (v. 3) _____ *Give praise to God* _____

2. (v. 4) _____

3. (v. 4) _____

4. (v. 5) _____

5. (v. 6) _____

6. (v. 6) _____

7. (v. 8) _____

My Assignment:
Cultivate a Thirsty Heart

The more you praise God, honor him in your attitudes and actions, pray to him, meditate on him, sing songs of joy to him, etc., the more you will cultivate a heart that is thirsty for God.

Your Assignment: This week, get together with a friend and increase your thirst for God.

Identify what you will do together here.

_____

_____

_____

_____

_____

_____

Week Four
Day 2
Week Four
Day 2
Week Four
Day 2
Week Four
Day 2
Week Four
Day 2
Week Four
Day 2
Week Four
Day 2
Week Four
Day 2
Week Four
Day 2
Week Four
Day 2
Week Four
Day 2
Week Four
Day 2
Week Four
Day 2
Week Four
Day 2
Week Four

Then note how your thirsty heart got even thirstier for God.

O Lord Almighty, happy are those who trust in you. (Psalm 84:12)

**Access your daily devotionals at www.MyCrossCulture.com/prayer or come back to this workbook for your daily devotional assignment.

Daily Devotional

Week Four
Days 3–5
Week Four
Days 3–5
Week Four
Days 3–5
Week Four
Days 3–5
Week Four
Days 3–5
Week Four
Days 3–5
Week Four
Days 3–5
Week Four
Days 3–5
Week Four
Days 3–5
Week Four
Days 3–5
Week Four
Days 3–5
Week Four
Days 3–5
Week Four
Days 3–5
Week Four
Days 3–5
Week Four
Days 3–5
Week Four
Days 3–5

Week 4 | Day 3

Read Psalm 84:10—12

When you live in right relationship with God, what does he do? Thank him for being that kind of God.

_____

_____

_____

_____

Week 4 | Day 4

Read 2 Corinthians 5:14—15

Identify something you can do or say today that reflects your new life in Christ that will please Christ.

_____

_____

_____

_____

Week 4 | Day 5

Read Philippians 1:6

You are one project God won't give up on. How does that make you feel? Let God know what he means to you today.

_____

_____

_____

_____

SECTION THREE
A Separated Life

Where Is the Power to Counter the Culture?

THE KEY to the CrossCulture life—the key to pleasing Christ with our lives—is not trying harder. In fact, the key is not trying at all.

The Bible says, in Galatians 5:22-23 (fill in the blanks):

> *But when _____ _____ _____ controls*
>
> *our lives, _____ will produce this kind of fruit in _____: love, joy, peace, patience, kindness, goodness, faithfulness, gentleness, and self-control. Here there is no conflict with the law. (Galatians 5:22-23)*

According to those verses, who or what will produce the things in your life that will please Christ? (check one)

○ eating my vegetables
○ trying really, really hard
○ the Holy Spirit
○ hoping for the best
○ my efforts
○ going to church

The Bible says, in Ephesians 3:16-17:

> *I pray that from his glorious, unlimited resources he will give you mighty inner strength through his Holy Spirit. And I pray that Christ will be more and more at home in your hearts as you trust in him. (Ephesians 3:16-17)*

Look up the following verses in your Bible. In each pair, circle the verse as it is found in the Bible and cross out the incorrect verse. Then answer the questions that follow.

GALATIANS 5:16:

> So I advise you to live according to your new life in the Holy Spirit. Then you won't be doing what your sinful nature craves.

> So I advise you to grit your teeth and try as hard as you can not to be doing what your sinful nature craves.

ROMANS 12:2:

> Don't copy the behavior and customs of this world, but instead transform yourself into a new person by really working hard at changing the way you think. Then you will know what God wants you to do, and you will know how good and pleasing and perfect his will really is.

> Don't copy the behavior and customs of this world, but let God transform you into a new person by changing the way you think. Then you will know what God wants you to do, and you will know how good and pleasing and perfect his will really is.

GALATIANS 2:19-20:

> I have been crucified with Christ. I myself no longer live, but Christ lives in me. So I live my life in this earthly body by working hard to please the Son of God, who loved me and gave himself for me.

> I have been crucified with Christ. I myself no longer live, but Christ lives in me. So I live my life in this earthly body by trusting in the Son of God, who loved me and gave himself for me.

1. How would you describe the difference between the two versions of those verses? (Record your thoughts below, then discuss as a group.)

_____

_____

_____

_____

_____

2. How (in practical terms) can you really live according to your new relationship with the Holy Spirit? (Record your thoughts below, then discuss as a group.)

_____

_____

_____

_____

_____

3. How (in practical terms) can you let God transform you into a new person by changing the way you think? What does that mean? (record your thoughts below, then discuss as a group)

_____

_____

_____

_____

_____

Week Five
Group Session 5
Week Five
Group Session 5
Week Five
Group Session 5
Week Five
Group Session 5
Week Five
Group Session 5
Week Five
Group Session 5
Week Five
Group Session 5
Week Five
Group Session 5
Week Five
Group Session 5
Week Five
Group Session 5
Week Five
Group Session 5
Week Five
Group Session 5
Week Five
Group Session 5
Week Five
Group Session 5

4. How (in practical terms) can you live your life in this earthly body by trusting in the Son of God? (record your thoughts below, then discuss as a group)

_____

_____

_____

_____

_____

5. Is that really any different from trying? (record your thoughts below, then discuss as a group)

_____

_____

_____

_____

_____

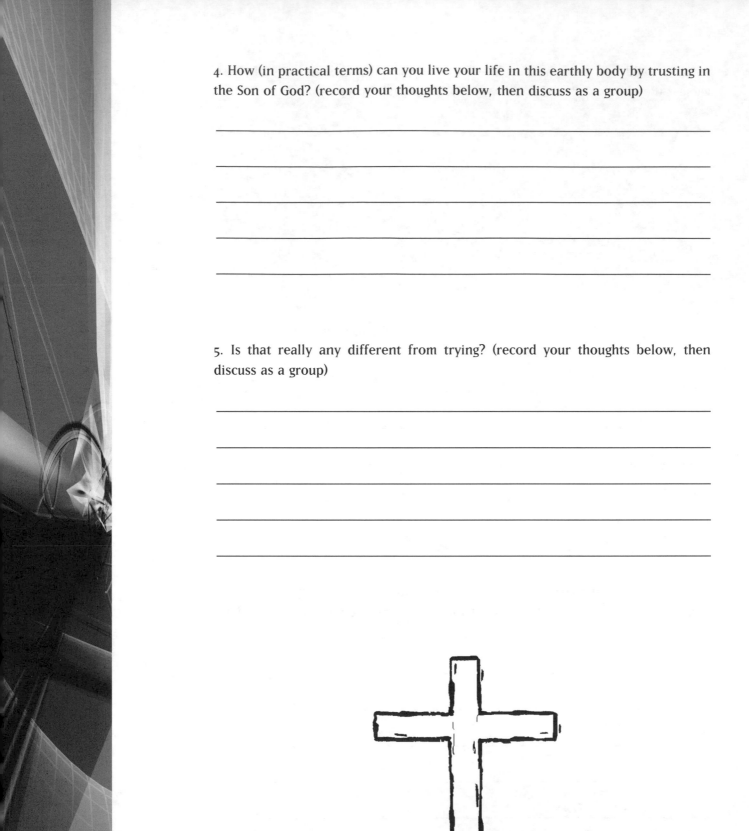

The Workout Can Avoid a Knockout

"BOB! WEAVE! FEINT!" the trainer commanded. "Now duck." It was too late. Jim's sparring partner landed a left cross that put him to the canvas.

"You've got to block that punch," the trainer said as Jim slowly got off the mat. Let's go at it again. You can win the fight next week if you master the techniques."

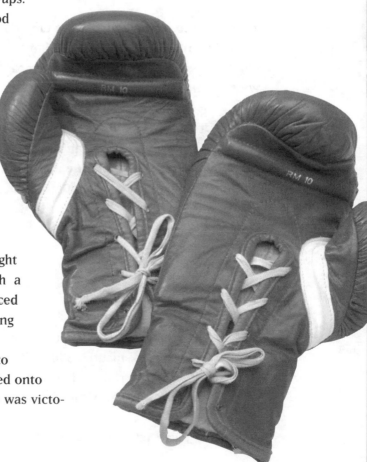

For weeks Jim had gone through a rigorous workout. Push-ups. Weight lifting. Sit-ups. Running. Punching bags. Sparring. Good diet. Up early—to bed late. Jim was giving his all to win the prize of "the Golden Glove" of amateur boxing.

The big night came. It was sixty seconds into the fourth round. Jim bobbed and weaved and feinted. The left cross came flying at him and he blocked it. With his opponent wide open, Jim responded with a left uppercut followed by a thunderous right hand. His opponent went down with a thud. The crowd cheered. Jim bounced back and forth waiting for the reeling boxer to get up. But he couldn't.

The referee waved his hands to signal the fight was over. And Jim leaped onto the ropes with his hands held high. He was victorious.

The Power to Live Right

THE POWER to overcome Jim's opponent came from what he did—the push-ups, the running, the footwork, eating right, and continued hard practice. But the Christian life is different. All your human efforts to live right will not bring victory.

Scripture teaches us that a Christian becomes a new person and the old life of practicing sinful behavior is to stop. Which means we are to somehow overcome the habits of the old life. Romans 12:2 says, "Don't copy the behavior and customs of the world."

But where does the power to overcome the old life come from? What is the real source of spiritual strength? Check (✓) the true or false statement below.

1. **Spiritual strength to overcome is a result of continual gritting your teeth and working harder to overcome sinful appetites.**

2. **The key to living a victorious Christian life is in sincerely believing you have what it takes deep within to live up to your potential.**

3. **It's not a matter of overcoming sinful behavior in your life, you can't do it. It's simply a matter of developing more willpower so you don't sin quite as much as you used to.**

Is self-effort the secret to a life of joy, love, peace, kindness, patience, goodness, and self-control that the Bible talks about? Is believing in yourself and your own potential the secret? Or is it really futile to even try, because overcoming sinful behavior is a never-ending battle?

READ JOHN 14:16-17 AND 26. Then answer the following questions.

What did Jesus say his Father would send? _____

Where will this person lead you? _____ (v. 17).

What will he teach you? _____ (v. 26).

Paul the apostle said, "I pray that from his glorious, unlimited resources he will give you mighty inner strength through his Holy Spirit" (Ephesians 3:16).

Sacrifice, laying aside our selfish ambitions, and discipline are part of the CrossCulture. But none of us has the power to live the Christian life in our own strength. It is the Holy Spirit that is our "unlimited resource." He is the one who gives us the inner strength.

Unleashing the Power

AT THIS POINT you might say: "If I have confessed my sins and trusted in Christ, my sins are forever nailed to the cross and God raises me to new life. Right? Now I am transformed from death to life. Then I am crucified with Christ so that my selfish life is starved and new nature is fed. Do I have that right so far? Okay. So presto, now I no longer "copy the behavior and customs of this world, but let God transform [me] into a new person by changing the way [I] think" (Romans 12:2). Sounds easy. But somewhere there's got to be a catch. There's something I've got to do? Right?"

Right. There *is* something we do. When we repent of our sins, God forgives us and raises us from life to death because of Christ's sacrificial death. We deny ourselves, take up our cross, and become a follower of Christ with God's Holy Spirit living inside us. But for his Holy Spirit to literally live through us and change our behavior, there *is* something we must do.

What is it? What do you think it is that enables the Holy Spirit to live his life through your life?

_____

_____

_____

_____

NOTE: If you are signed up at the MyCrossCulture e-prayer group, please go online to complete the rest of this lesson.

Week Five
Day 1
Week Five
Day 1
Week Five
Day 1
Week Five
Day 1
Week Five
Day 1
Week Five
Day 1
Week Five
Day 1
Week Five
Day 1
Week Five
Day 1
Week Five
Day 1
Week Five
Day 1
Week Five
Day 1
Week Five
Day 1
Week Five

Continue on with this workbook if you do not wish to complete this lesson online.

A Relationship That Yields

READ these passages thoughtfully.

Do not let any part of your body become a tool of wickedness, to be used for sinning. Instead, give yourselves completely to God since you have been given new life. And use your whole body as a tool to do what is right for the glory of God. Sin is no longer your master, for you are no longer subject to the law, which enslaves you to sin. Instead, you are free by God's grace. (Romans 6:13-14)

And so, dear Christian friends, I plead with you to give your bodies to God. Let them be a living and holy sacrifice—the kind he will accept. When you think of what he has done, is this too much to ask? (Romans 12:1)

After reading these passages, do you have a different answer to "*What it is that enables the Holy Spirit to live his life through your life?*" If so, write your new answer here:

_____

_____

_____

_____

_____

_____

Romans 6 says, "Give yourself completely to God." Romans 12 says, "Give your bodies to God. Let them be a living and holy sacrifice." Identify words below that reflect a giving relationship with God. (Check (✓) those that you think apply.)

- ○ I work harder at being better.
- ○ I submit to his wishes.
- ○ I release to his control.
- ○ I follow his leading.
- ○ I make myself do right.
- ○ I endure more on my own.
- ○ I take control of my life.
- ○ I yield to what he wants.

The secret to living the Christian life is in giving yourself to the one you love—the Lord Jesus Christ. A love relationship causes you to care what he thinks, it submits to his control, allowing him to direct you and yield to his ways. It is a relationship in which you submit to him that unleashes his power through you to live like him.

Jesus said:

> *"If you love me, obey my commandments. . . . Those who obey my commandments are the ones who love me." (John 14:15, 21)*

Is obedience to Jesus a requirement or a result of your relationship? Explain.

_____

_____

_____

_____

When we focus on obedience to Scripture and doing right outside of our relationship with Christ, it can lead to legalism (obeying for obedience's sake). But when we focus on our love relationship with Christ and making him more at home in our hearts, obedience is an empowered result because we are yielding to his control.

> *When the Holy Spirit controls our lives, he will produce this kind of fruit in us: love, joy, peace, patience, kindness, goodness, faithfulness, gentleness and self-control...If we are living now by the Holy Spirit, let us follow the Holy Spirit's leading in every part of our lives. (Galatians 5:22-23, 25)*

My Assignment: Create My Prayer

A LOVE RELATIONSHIP with Christ that yields, submits, and surrenders completely to God isn't that much to ask when you stop and think about what he has done for you. Where would you be without God? Think of the benefits in your life because of your relationship with Christ.

Tell God right now where you would be without him and how much you want to give yourself to him today and every day.

Week Five
Day 1
Week Five
Day 1
Week Five
Day 1
Week Five
Day 1
Week Five
Day 1
Week Five
Day 1
Week Five
Day 1
Week Five
Day 1
Week Five
Day 1
Week Five
Day 1
Week Five
Day 1
Week Five

Dear God

_____

_____

_____

_____

_____

_____

Let your group know your heartfelt prayer to God and ask them to pray that you will consistently yield to the one who empowers you with real life. Respond to their requests and let them know you're praying for them.

> *Now you are free from the power of sin and have become slaves of God. Now you do those things that lead to holiness and result in eternal life. (Romans 6:22)*

How To Make Christ Welcome

The Welcome Test

HOW DO THE following situations make you feel? Place a check (✓) in the circle that best represents how you feel.

When someone looks right at me and appears attentive when I am talking I feel . . .

1. ◯ Disgusted
2. ◯ Silly
3. ◯ Listened to

When friends notice me when I enter a room and let me know they are glad I'm there I feel . . .

1. ◯ Sick
2. ◯ Hungry
3. ◯ Appreciated

When a crowd acknowledges an achievement I have made I feel . . .

1. ◯ Sleepy
2. ◯ Tired
3. ◯ Honored

When people let me know my thoughts and views are important to them I feel . . .

1. ◯ Sorry
2. ◯ Ugly
3. ◯ Respected

Now add up the numbers beside each box you checked. What is your score? If you scored less than 12 you probably have a fever and are too sick to complete this lesson. Seriously, we all feel more welcome and loved when we're listened to, appreciated, honored, and respected. But here's the key question:

Do we need to adjust to, cater to, or accommodate the needs or interests of the other person in order to make them truly feel welcome?

○ Yes   ○ No

Yielding, submitting, and allowing God the Holy Spirit to control your life is really about making Christ at home in your life. That's what a love relationship with Christ does. To make Christ welcome in your heart, you must accommodate him, adjust to his likes and dislikes, and understand what it is that pleases him.

> *I pray that from his glorious, unlimited resources he will give you mighty inner strength through his Holy Spirit. And I pray that Christ will be more and more at home in your hearts as you trust in him. (Ephesians 3:16-17)*

The amazing thing is when you sacrifice yourself in some way to accommodate Christ his Holy Spirit in turn empowers you to live in obedience to him.

Yield and Welcome Exercise

LET'S IDENTIFY some practical areas of your life this week in which you could yield some aspect of yourself to Christ that would make him feel more at home in your life.

Think of someone who isn't your best friend, someone who may not even like you. What could you do this week that would demonstrate an act of kindness toward them?

_____

_____

_____

How would this act of kindness cause you to deny yourself or follow the Holy Spirit's leading?

_____

_____

_____

READ MATTHEW 5:38-40.

Do you sense Christ would be more at home in your heart by performing this act of kindness on someone that isn't a very good friend? How?

_____

_____

_____

_____

Think of someone in need. Perhaps a friend who's sick, a grandparent who's lonely, a student in need of help with homework, a neighbor who needs a lawn mowed, etc. What could you do this week that could lift a load for someone that would bring a smile to God's face?

_____

_____

_____

_____

How would lifting a load from another put you out or inconvenience you? What would this deny you?

_____

_____

_____

_____

Read Matthew 25:35-40.

Would inconveniencing yourself to help another make Christ feel more at home in your heart? Why?

_____

_____

_____

_____

Week Five
Day 2
Week Five
Day 2
Week Five
Day 2
Week Five
Day 2
Week Five
Day 2
Week Five
Day 2
Week Five
Day 2
Week Five
Day 2
Week Five
Day 2
Week Five
Day 2
Week Five
Day 2
Week Five
Day 2
Week Five
Day 2
Week Five

Think of one or both of your parents. They have no doubt cared for you for all these years. Are they perfect parents? Probably not. But they are parents who need to be honored. What could you do or say this week that would show them honor? How about writing them a note expressing how much you appreciate them, respect them, and need them? Write your note here.

_____

_____

_____

_____

_____

_____

_____

Is expressing your deep felt honor toward either parent different? Why? Do you sense you will need to yield to God's leadings?

_____

_____

_____

_____

READ EXODUS 20:12.

How do you sense Christ feels about you showing honor to your parents?

_____

_____

_____

My Assignment:
Honor My Parents This Week

IF ONE OR MORE of your parents are in the MyCrossCulture e-prayer group, go to the site and send them the note you prepared. You can send them the note in the same way as you post your prayers. You could also send an e-mail or write out the note and give it to them.

One thing is certain. When you resist any tendency of not wanting to do this assignment and do it anyway—God smiles. He is pleased and Christ is made more welcome in your heart, when in obedience you express honor to your parents.

Come back to this page after you have expressed honor to your parent(s) and write down how they responded.

_____

_____

_____

_____

_____

Feel free to complete the other exercises this week of reaching out to someone in need or showing an act of kindness to a not-so-good "friend."

**Access your daily devotional at MyCrossCulture.com/prayer or come back to this workbook for our daily devotional assignments.

Week Five
Day 2
Week Five
Day 2
Week Five
Day 2
Week Five
Day 2
Week Five
Day 2
Week Five
Day 2
Week Five
Day 2
Week Five
Day 2
Week Five
Day 2
Week Five
Day 2
Week Five
Day 2
Week Five
Day 2
Week Five
Day 2
Week Five
Day 2
Week Five
Day 2
Week Five

Daily Devotional

Week 5 | Day 3

Read Galatians 5:16—18

The old sinful nature is not your friend. Its desires do not lead to happiness and meaning. What must you do today to unleash God's power to live according to your new life in Christ?

_____

_____

_____

_____

Week 5 | Day 4

Read Galatians 5:22—23

Pick a fruit of the Spirit and ask God to empower you to exhibit it today. Which one did you pick? How will you express it?

_____

_____

_____

_____

Week 5 | Day 5

Read James 1:5—8

Whom does God show favor to? Ask God to empower you with that quality today.

_____

_____

_____

_____

The Secret to Your Purpose in Life

Week 6 | Group Session 6

GOD'S PLAN is to not only to transform us to new life, but also to continually transform us more and more into his likeness.

The Bible says, in 2 Corinthians 3:18 (NIV):

> *And we, who with unveiled faces all reflect the Lord's glory, are being transformed into his likeness with ever-increasing glory, which comes from the Lord, who is the Spirit (2 Corinthians 3:18, NIV).*

God designed tadpoles to become frogs. He designed caterpillars to metamorphose into butterflies. He created acorns to be transformed into mighty oaks.

Similarly, according to the Bible, we were all meant to possess the likeness of God—righteous, holy, and true. That likeness was spoiled by sin, but when we experience the transformation of becoming new creations in Jesus Christ (see 2 Corinthians 5:17), we recover the ability to "be mirrors that brightly reflect the glory of the Lord. And as the Spirit of the Lord works within us, we become more and more like him and reflect his glory even more" (2 Corinthians 3:18). "For God knew his people in advance, and he chose them to become like his Son" (Romans 8:29).

So we are meant to become like Christ . . . that is our destiny.

Week Six
Group Session 6
Week Six
Group Session 6
Week Six
Group Session 6
Week Six
Group Session 6
Week Six
Group Session 6
Week Six
Group Session 6
Week Six
Group Session 6
Week Six
Group Session 6
Week Six
Group Session 6
Week Six
Group Session 6
Week Six
Group Session 6
Week Six
Group Session 6
Week Six
Group Session 6

To Know Me Is to Love Me

Love?

IMAGINE Bobby Lee, a "love struck" boy, taking pretty little Mary Lou out on a date. Is this true love?

"I'm glad we're going out again, Mary Lou," Bobby Lee said, pulling out of the driveway. "I sure do like you a lot."

"Thank you, Bobby Lee," Mary Lou said as she fastened her seatbelt. "I like you, too."

"Yeah, I really do like going out with you," Bobby Lee said, "because of the great restaurants we get to go to with your dad's credit card. It's really nice of him to let you use it like that."

"Yeah, I know, Bobby Lee," she said.

"And I like the crowd we run with. I mean, you're so popular and all, I've got every guy in school envying me."

"Yeah, I know, Bobby Lee," Mary Lou answered flatly.

"And it's great," Bobby Lee continued, "that you're so pretty, because who wants to date some dorky-looking girl? I mean, the guys would make fun of me, you know?"

"Yeah, I know, Bobby Lee."

"And it's great—" he continued, but Mary Lou interrupted.

"Yeah, I know, Bobby Lee, you really like Dad's car, too."

"Yeah, how did you know I was going to say that, Mary Lou?"

"Bobby Lee?" she asked.

"Yes, Mary Lou?"

"You haven't said anything about all the letters and notes I've been writing to you. Do you like getting my letters?"

"Oh, I sure do, Mary Lou! They smell so good!"

"Well," she continued, "can we talk about some of them? I mean, I've written you sixty-six letters, you know. And Bobby Lee, you've never said a thing about a single one of them."

"Well, I'd like to talk about them, Mary Lou, I surely would . . . but . . . but . . . well, you see, it's like this," he said. "I haven't really read them yet."

"You what?" Mary Lou answered, spinning around to stare at him. "You haven't read them?"

"Well, now, Mary Lou, you've got to understand," he said, running a finger under the collar of his shirt. "I'm really busy with schoolwork and football practice and video games and e-mailing my friends and—"

"But, Bobby Lee, I poured my heart out to you in those letters. I told you all sorts of personal things in them, things I truly wanted you to know. I told you about all my favorite things and things I don't like and...and my fears and all my dreams." She paused, and her voice dropped. "So where are my letters?"

"Oh, oh, you'll really be pleased, Mary Lou," Bobby Lee said. "I've saved every one, I really have. I keep them in a special place, don't you worry about that."

A long silence followed, until finally Bobby Lee spoke again.

"Mary Lou . . . I really do love you, though," he said softly.

"But, Bobby Lee," she answered, looking sorrowfully at him. "You . . . you don't even know me."

What God Wants

THERE ARE A number of things you could say that God wants. Complete these sentences of what you think God wants of us.

1. God wants us to _____ him.

2. God wants us to _____ others.

3. God wants the world to be _____ .

God desires many things for us, of course, but some are more important to him than others. Fill in the missing word in the verse that follows:

God says: "I want you to be merciful; I don't want your sacrifices.

I want you to _____ God; that's more important than burnt offering." (Hosea 6:6)

Without looking up the verse, you might have filled in the blank with the word *love*. God certainly wants you to love him with all your heart, soul, and mind. But loving devotion doesn't mean much unless it draws two individuals together in an intimate knowledge of each other. God is passionate about a relationship with us—he wants us to *know him.*

What do you know about God? We know he is all-powerful and all-knowing. God is perfect and eternal. But based on your general knowledge, list five things that you know about God's character and nature. What is God like as revealed in the person of Jesus Christ?

> • Christ is _____
>
> • Christ is _____
>
> • Christ is _____
>
> • Christ is _____
>
> • Christ is _____

Which of the qualities you listed above does God want you to display? Check (✓) one that applies.

    ○ none of them   ○ some of them   ○ all of them

There must be a spiritual renewal of your thoughts and attitudes. You must display a new nature because you are a new person created in God's likeness—righteous, holy, and true. (Ephesians 4:23-24)

It is God's plan that you become Christlike—a reflection of what Jesus Christ is like. That is your destiny, for "he chose [you] to become like his Son" (Romans 8:29). But how? So far in this workbook what have we discovered about the Cross-Culture life that helps answer that?

• You were dead to God because of sin.
• Christ's death on the cross paid for that sin.
• Through repentance and trust in Christ, you were transformed from death to life.

Week Six
Day 1
Week Six
Day 1
Week Six
Day 1
Week Six
Day 1
Week Six
Day 1
Week Six
Day 1
Week Six
Day 1
Week Six
Day 1
Week Six
Day 1
Week Six
Day 1
Week Six
Day 1
Week Six
Day 1
Week Six
Day 1
Week Six

• You now have a committed relationship with God in which you lay aside your selfish ambitions, take up your cross, and follow Christ.

By yielding to God, his Holy Spirit empowers you to live cross-grained to the culture. Welcoming Christ in your life and making him "more and more at home" *does* begin to change your life. Yet that change is based upon your growing knowledge of Christ.

> *You have clothed yourself with a brand-new nature that is continually being renewed as you learn more and more about Christ, who created this new nature within you. (Colossians 3:10)*

Fill in the blanks based on the verse above.

My new nature is _____ being renewed.

That renewal is based upon me learning _____

_____   _____ about Christ.

Christ is the one who _____ this new nature within me.

NOTE: Go to your MyCrossCulture e-prayer group site to complete the rest of this lesson if you are taking advantage of the online prayer group. Otherwise, continue on with this written lesson.

It's Who You Know, Not What You Know

IS KNOWLEDGE of what Christ is like the real issue? If we study Scripture and learn all the qualities of Christ, will that make us like Christ?

○ yes   ○ no

> *While knowledge may make us feel important, it is love that really builds up the church. Anyone who claims to know all the answers doesn't really know very much. But the person who loves God is the one God knows and cares for. (1 Corinthians 8:1-3)*

The purpose of knowing Jesus better is . . . Check (✓) all that apply.

knowing Jesus!

○ to be biblically knowledgeable
○ to be more like Christ
○ to honor and glorify God
○ to show others you know what you're talking about
○ to love him even more

Read this passage carefully:

As we know Jesus better, his divine power gives us everything we need for living a godly life. He has called us to receive his own glory and goodness! . . . He has promised that you will escape the decadence all around you caused by evil desires and that you will share in his divine nature. (2 Peter 1:3-4)

Second Peter 1 says living a godly life is based on what two things? "As we

_____ _____ _____, his _____ _____

gives us everything we need for living a godly life (v. 3).

The process is clear. The more we love Christ, the more we will make him at home in our lives. The more we make him at home, the more we will come to know him. The more we know him, the more we will be like him.

In fact, that is the very *purpose* for which we live: *To love and know God so we can be more and more like him.*

My Assignment: Create My Prayer

PAUL THE APOSTLE was from a pure-blooded Jewish family. He demanded strict obedience to the Jewish law for himself and others. And yet, here is what he said:

I once thought all these things were so very important, but now I consider them worthless because of what Christ has done. Yes, everything is worthless when compared with the priceless gain of knowing Christ Jesus my Lord. I have discarded everything else, counting it all garbage, so that I may know Christ and become one with him. (Philippians 3:7-9)

Express your heart's desire in your own words—how you want to know Christ for who he really is. Let him know you want to fulfill your purpose to love and know him so you can be more like him.

Week Six
Day 1
Week Six
Day 1
Week Six
Day 1
Week Six
Day 1
Week Six
Day 1
Week Six
Day 1
Week Six
Day 1
Week Six
Day 1
Week Six
Day 1
Week Six
Day 1
Week Six
Day 1
Week Six
Day 1
Week Six
Day 1
Week Six

Dear Lord

_____

_____

_____

_____

_____

_____

_____

_____

Post your prayer for your group members to pray for you. Be sure to let them know you're praying for them. It would be good to let your parents know how this course is helping you. Why don't you include them in your requests for prayer.

I can really know Christ and experience the mighty power that raised him from the dead. (Philippians 3:10)

Imagine the Imaginable

IMAGINE THIS. While you are reading these very words, everything around you falls silent. The room you are in vanishes and a soft blue glow is all you see before you. Then you hear the most beautiful voice you have ever heard. It is a deep resonant tone, so pleasant yet so majestic you gasp for breath.

"I am the Alpha and the Omega," the voice begins, "the beginning and the end. I am the one who is, who always was, and is still to come, the Almighty One."

Your spine tingles but you move not a muscle, for you realize the voice you are hearing is the voice of God.

"I am the infinite one who knows no boundaries or limitations. My power and knowledge and greatness are beyond your comprehension. My love and holiness and beauty are so intense that to see me in all my glory would overwhelm you—for as a mortal you could not see me and live. And yet . . . I created you to know me intimately, for I am passionate about my relationship with you.

"I know everything there is to know about you. I know your favorite color, your favorite food, what music you like, the dreams you have, and the future you long for. I know your struggles and weaknesses. I am glad with you when you make right choices. I am saddened when you make wrong choices. I know you better than you know yourself, and . . . *I long for you to know me.*"

Increasing Your Hunger

YOU SNAP out of it. The voice is gone but the truth remains. God wants you to know him . . . so much so that he revealed himself in human form so you could truly relate to him.

How does it make you feel to know that the Almighty God of the universe wants you to get to know him? Check (✓) all those that apply.

Week Six
Day 2
Week Six
Day 2
Week Six
Day 2
Week Six
Day 2
Week Six
Day 2
Week Six
Day 2
Week Six
Day 2
Week Six
Day 2
Week Six
Day 2
Week Six
Day 2
Week Six
Day 2
Week Six

○ Humbled
○ Dizzy
○ Honored
○ Sore
○ Wanted
○ Amazed
○ Grateful
○ Valued
○ Sticky
○ Accepted

Knowing God!

As we stated before, the more and more we know Christ, the more we will be like him and live according to his ways.

> *I reflect at night on who you are, O Lord,*
>   *and I obey your law because of this. (Psalm 119:55)*

Who is Christ? What is he like? The more you know him the more you will love him, because he is the essence of love itself. "Anyone who does not love does not know God—for God is love" (1 John 4:8).

So if we knew what love (God's love) was like, we would have a good place to start in knowing what Christ was like. To put that in writing, let's go to 1 Corinthians 13 and replace the word *love* with the word *Christ*. This will give us a clearer picture of Christ.

Fill in the blanks from 1 Corinthians 13:4-8 printed below. The first is completed for you as an example.

- Christ is _____*patient*_____ and _____.

- Christ is not _____ or _____

  or _____ or _____.

- Christ does not _____ his _____

  _____ .

- Christ is not _____ and he keeps

  _____ _____ of when he has been wronged.

- Christ is never glad about _____ but rejoices whenever the truth wins out.

- Christ never _____ _____, never loses

    _____ , he is always _____ and

    _____ through every circumstance.

- Christ will _____ _____.

Love is patient and kind. Love is not jealous or boastful or proud or rude. Love does not demand its own way. Love is not irritable, and it keeps no record of when it has been wronged. It is never glad about injustice but rejoices whenever the truth wins out. Love never gives up, never loses faith, is always hopeful, and endures through every circumstance. Love will last forever. (1 Corinthians 13:4-8)

Can you sense Christ saying to you: "Learn how patient and kind I am and you will love me. Come to know my mercy and my faithfulness and you will love me. Know that I see the deepest, darkest secrets of your life, things you are ashamed of, and I love and accept you regardless, and you will love me in return. You can love me because I first loved you."

Take the time right now and read Psalm 63:1-8 and keep your Bible open.

Does your soul thirst for God, and your very being long to know him as he is?

Based on Psalm 63:3, what does your love and hunger for God cause you to do?

_____

_____

Based on verse 4, what are you prompted to do?

_____

_____

Based on verse 5, what are you motivated to do?

_____

_____

Week Six
Day 2
Week Six
Day 2
Week Six
Day 2
Week Six
Day 2
Week Six
Day 2
Week Six
Day 2
Week Six
Day 2
Week Six
Day 2
Week Six
Day 2
Week Six
Day 2
Week Six
Day 2
Week Six
Day 2
Week Six
Day 2
Week Six

Based on verse 6. what are you encouraged to do?

_____

_____

My Assignment: Live It!

IT IS TRUE that knowing Jesus better "gives us everything we need for living a godly life" (2 Peter 1:3). But it is also true that your trust and faith in God "will produce a life of moral excellence. A life of moral excellence leads to knowing God better. Knowing God leads to self-control" (2 Peter 1:5-6). So the more you live out your passion for God, the more your passion and hunger for him will increase.

Contemplate a quality of Christ that you want to reflect this week and write it out here.

_____

_____

_____

_____

_____

_____

Now be intentional about reflecting him in your life this week. Come back here or on your CrossCulture Web site and journal what happens.

_____

_____

_____

_____

_____

_____

This week . . .

May your roots go down deep into the soil of God's marvelous love. And may you have the power to understand, as all God's people should, how wide, how long, how high, and how deep his love really is. May you experience the love of Christ, though it is so great you will never fully understand it. Then you will be filled with the fullness of life and power that comes from God. (Ephesians 3:17-19)

**Go to www.MyCrossCulture.com/prayer to access your devotionals or come back to this workbook for your daily devotional assignment.

Week Six
Day 2
Week Six
Day 2
Week Six
Day 2
Week Six
Day 2
Week Six
Day 2
Week Six
Day 2
Week Six
Day 2
Week Six
Day 2
Week Six
Day 2
Week Six
Day 2
Week Six
Day 2
Week Six
Day 2
Week Six
Day 2
Week Six

Daily Devotional

Week 6 Day 3

Read 2 Corinthians 3:12—18

Would you like your mirror to more brightly reflect the glory of Christ? Identify how you can become more like him today and yield to his Spirit.

_____

_____

_____

_____

Week 6 Day 4

Read 2 Peter 1:3—4

Whose nature do you share in and what does that give you?

_____

_____

_____

_____

Week 6 Day 5

Read Philippians 3:7—11

Do you long to know him? He longs for you to know him and to be your best friend. Let him hear you tell him you want to know him for who he really is. Dear Lord . . .

_____

_____

_____

_____

SECTION FOUR

A Mission In Life

Your Special Mission

THE CROSSCULTURE LIFE, which we've been talking about these last several weeks, is also a life that has been given a clear and compelling mission.

Three verses that talk about your mission are scrambled in the columns below. In your group session this week, you'll learn what the proper order of the words below really is:

2 CORINTHIANS 5:18:

what	God,	newness
of	life	reconciling
brought	God	back
people	to	who
task	himself	through
given	Christ	the
And	this	has
All	us	did.
to	us	is
from	of	him.

Write the corrected verse below:

_____

_____

_____

_____

_____

2 CORINTHIANS 5:19:

the	us	sins
in	people's	wonderful
is	world	to
message	Christ,	longer
counting	them.	was
tell	the	to
For	no	has
himself,	he	reconciling
given	God	This
against	others.	

Write the corrected verse below:

_____

_____

_____

_____

_____

2 CORINTHIANS 5:20:

to	pleading	us
you,	"Be	God
is	as	reconciled
to	speak	to
you.	We	were
you,	using	though
Christ	are	urge
We	himself	with
ambassadors,	and	Christ's
here	God!	

Write the corrected verse below:

_____

_____

_____

_____

_____

What are some of the practical, real-life ways we can be Christ's ambassadors? Cross out what you consider to be incorrect answers below:

1. **LOVE ONE ANOTHER.** *"Love each other. Just as I have loved you, you should love each other. Your love for each other will prove to the world that you are my disciples"* (John 13:34-35, NLT).

2. **RAISE RABBITS.** *"Thus do we all, like Peter Cottontail, show regard one for the other"* (2 Beatrix 4:7, TLC).

3. **EXCEL IN SPORTS.** *"For all who can hit a baseball, catch a football, sink a three-pointer, or score a goal, these will people listen to and esteem above all others"* (1 Hesitations 12:1, ATV).

4. **DO KIND AND GOOD THINGS.** *"Be careful to do good deeds all the time"* (Titus 2:7, NLT).

5. **ENDURE HARDSHIP AND PERSECUTION.** *"Endure suffering along with me, as a good soldier of Christ Jesus"* (2 Timothy 2:3, NLT).

Week Seven
Group Session 7
Week Seven
Group Session 7
Week Seven
Group Session 7
Week Seven
Group Session 7
Week Seven
Group Session 7
Week Seven
Group Session 7
Week Seven
Group Session 7
Week Seven
Group Session 7
Week Seven
Group Session 7
Week Seven
Group Session 7
Week Seven
Group Session 7
Week Seven
Group Session 7
Week Seven
Group Session 7
Week Seven

6. LIVE RIGHTEOUSLY. *"Live clean, innocent lives as children of God in a dark world full of crooked and perverse people. Let your lives shine brightly before them"* (Philippians 2:15, NLT).

7. SAY AS LITTLE AS POSSIBLE. *"Children should be seen and not heard"* (Malarkians 9:45, BLT).

8. JOIN THE CIRCUS. *"Let all who enter be encouraged and uplifted by the daring young men on the flying trapeze"* (Balaam 21:8, SUV).

9. BE READY TO EXPLAIN YOUR FAITH. *"And if you are asked about your Christian hope, always be ready to explain it"* (1 Peter 3:15, NLT).

10. WATCH LESS TELEVISION. *"For all that is in the world, the lust of the flesh, and the lust of the eyes, and the pride of life, is found on television"* (1 John 2:16, KJV).

We try to live in such a way that no one will be hindered from finding the Lord by the way we act, and so no one can find fault with our ministry. (2 Corinthians 6:3)

Chosen

SAM WAS A GOOD KID. He avoided the bad crowd and did his best to stay out of trouble. He didn't live with his parents. The local minister, Pastor E, had taken him in.

One night while Sam was in his room sleeping, he thought he heard someone call out his name. So he got up and found Pastor E in his study. "Is everything okay, Pastor?" Sam asked.

"Everything's fine, Sam," the pastor responded.

Sam went back to bed. But before long, Sam heard someone call out his name again. This time he was sure he wasn't dreaming. He got up and went to Pastor E's room. "Okay, what do you want?" Sam asked.

"I don't want anything."

"But you called me, didn't you?" Sam asked.

"No," Pastor E answered. "I didn't call you. Go back to bed, Sam."

By this time, Sam was totally confused. But the pastor gave no indication he was playing a joke on him, so Sam simply scratched his head and went back to bed. Only moments later, it happened again. A clear voice rang out: "Sam, Sam," it called.

There was no mistake. Sam quickly ran to Pastor E's room and told the man what had been happening.

By now, you probably recognize the story as something that really happened. In fact, it's recorded in the Bible. Here is how Scripture finishes the story:

> *Eli realized it was the Lord who was calling the boy. So he said to Samuel, "Go and lie down again and if someone calls again, say, 'Yes, Lord, your servant is listening.'" So Samuel went back to bed.*
>
> *And the Lord came and called as before, "Samuel! Samuel!"*
>
> *And Samuel replied, "Yes, your servant is listening." (1 Samuel 3:8-10)*

Who You Gonna Call?

THROUGHOUT HISTORY, God called people to various tasks and as servants of God they listened. (Fill in the blanks with the names of some people God called; the first one has been done for you.)

• When God wanted to raise up a new priesthood, whom did he call?
_____Samuel_____

• When God wanted to destroy evil with a flood, yet save a righteous family and the animals of the earth, whom did he call? _____ (see Genesis 6).

• When God wanted to save Jacob's family from famine, what dreamer did he call? _____ (see Genesis 47).

• When God wanted to free his enslaved people from an Egyptian Pharaoh, whom did he call? _____ (see Exodus 3).

• When God wanted to kill Goliath the Philistine, whom did he call? _____ (see 1 Samuel 17).

Throughout the ages, God has called one person after another to accomplish his purpose. Yet perhaps his most significant call came to a man over six thousand years ago. His name was Abram. God appeared to him and said:

> *"I am God Almighty; serve me faithfully and live a blameless life. I will make a covenant with you, by which I will guarantee to make you into a mighty nation." At this, Abram fell face down in the dust. Then God said to him, "This is my covenant with you: I will make you the father of not just one nation, but a multitude of nations! What's more, I am changing your name. It will no longer be Abram; now you will be known as Abraham, for you will be the father of many nations. I will give you millions of descendants who will represent many nations. Kings will be among them!*
>
> *"I will continue this everlasting covenant between us, generation after generation. It will continue between me and your offspring forever. And I will always be your God and the God of your descendants after you." (Genesis 17:1-7)*

What nation are the descendants of Abraham? Check (✓) your answer below.

- ○ The Nation of Islam
- ○ The Nation of Israel
- ○ The United Nations
- ○ The United States of America

Who was the most significant person to be born from the descendants of Abraham, Isaac, and Jacob? Check (✓) your answer below.

- ○ Abraham Lincoln
- ○ Jesus of Nazareth
- ○ Isaac Newton
- ○ Mohammad
- ○ Michael Jackson
- ○ Jacob Marley

Is the Messiah, the Savior of the world, to be born out of the nation you checked above?

○ yes   ○ no   ○ not sure

Week Seven
Day 1
Week Seven
Day 1
Week Seven
Day 1
Week Seven
Day 1
Week Seven
Day 1
Week Seven
Day 1
Week Seven
Day 1
Week Seven
Day 1
Week Seven
Day 1
Week Seven
Day 1
Week Seven
Day 1
Week Seven
Day 1
Week Seven
Day 1
Week Seven
Day 1
Week Seven

So is it this nation that is supposed to be proclaiming the good news of salvation to all the people of the earth? Why or why not?

_____

_____

_____

_____

The Secret Plan

FOR CENTURIES, the Jewish nation, the descendants of Abraham, Isaac, and Jacob, have been God's channel to reveal himself to the world. His covenant was, and still is, with the children of Israel, promising that he will be their God forever. After sin entered the world, God promised to send them a Messiah who would usher in a kingdom that would overcome fighting, oppression, fear, and death and make the entire earth once more into a pristine garden, where everyone would live together in peace forever (see Isaiah 11 and 35).

If you are not a part of that nation, do you have such a promise from God? Why or why not?

_____

_____

_____

_____

For thousands of years, it was understood that God's promise was only for his people—the people of Israel. Then, some two thousand years ago, Paul the apostle, inspired by the Holy Spirit, wrote: "God's secret plan has now been revealed to us" (Ephesians 1:9).

> *And this is the secret plan: The Gentiles have an equal share with the Jews in all the riches inherited by God's children. Both groups have believed the Good News, and both are part of the same body and enjoy together the promise of blessings through Christ Jesus. By God's special favor and mighty power, I have been given the wonderful privilege of serving him by spreading this Good News. (Ephesians 3:6-7)*

God had a secret plan, a plan that existed from the very beginning of time, to extend the promise of blessing—an eternal inheritance—to everyone through Christ.

READ EPHESIANS 1:22-23.

God has put the authority of all things under whom? _____
(see Ephesians 1:22)

And God gave Christ authority for whose benefit? _____
(see Ephesians 1:22)

And the church is _____ body. (see Ephesians 1:23)

> *Together as one body, Christ reconciled both groups [Jew and Gentile] to God by means of [Christ's] death. (Ephesians 2:16)*

Who has the great opportunity and responsibility, not only to share in God's inheritance, but to spread the news that Christ came to raise dead hearts to new life in him?

_____

> *This is the wonderful message he has given us to tell others. We are Christ's ambassadors, and God is using us to speak to you. (2 Corinthians 5:19-20).*

NOTE: Go now your MyCrossCulture e-prayer group site to complete the rest of this workbook. Continue on here if you are not signed up to access the site.

Week Seven
Day 1
Week Seven
Day 1
Week Seven
Day 1
Week Seven
Day 1
Week Seven
Day 1
Week Seven
Day 1
Week Seven
Day 1
Week Seven
Day 1
Week Seven
Day 1
Week Seven
Day 1
Week Seven
Day 1
Week Seven
Day 1
Week Seven
Day 1
Week Seven
Day 1
Week Seven

The Call

GOD WAS counting on the descendants of Abraham to be God's ambassadors. However, many have rejected Jesus, their Messiah. But God had a secret plan. That plan was to make all those who trusted in Christ as their Messiah and Savior to become his ambassadors, or personal representatives. Prior to Christ coming to earth, that responsibility was solely in the hands of God's chosen people. Now the body of Christ—his Church—shares in that great call.

How does it feel for God to call you out to be his personal representative to the world?

_____

_____

_____

_____

_____

_____

_____

You might be tempted to respond as Jeremiah the prophet when he first realized God was calling him to be his "spokesman to the world." Here is the conversation he had with God. Does this sound anything like you?

> The Lord gave me a message. He said, "I knew you before I formed you in your mother's womb. Before you were born I set you apart and appointed you as my spokesman to the world."

> "O Sovereign Lord," I said, "I can't speak for you! I'm too young!"

> "Don't say that," the Lord replied, "for you must go wherever I send you and say whatever I tell you. And don't be afraid of the people, for I will be with you and take care of you. I, the Lord, have spoken!"

> Then the Lord touched my mouth and said, "See, I have put my words in your mouth!" (Jeremiah 1:4-9)

My Assignment: Create My Prayer

GOD HAS CALLED you to be his representative because you are part of his body—his church. He promises, as he did with Jeremiah, to be with you and care for you. In fact, he wants you to be a reflection of himself to the world—a speaking and living witness of him every day.

Talk to God right now and express your desire to be his representative. If you have any fear or reluctance in being his witness, tell him about it. Ask him to help you overcome anything that would hinder you from fulfilling your mission.

Dear God

_____

_____

_____

_____

_____

_____

_____

Let your group know your prayer and ask them to pray for you. Be sure and pray for them as they forward their requests to you.

> *Live clean, innocent lives as children of God in a dark world full of crooked and perverse people. Let your lives shine brightly before them. (Philippians 2:15)*

Week Seven
Day 1
Week Seven
Day 1
Week Seven
Day 1
Week Seven
Day 1
Week Seven
Day 1
Week Seven
Day 1
Week Seven
Day 1
Week Seven
Day 1
Week Seven
Day 1
Week Seven
Day 1
Week Seven
Day 1
Week Seven
Day 1
Week Seven
Day 1
Week Seven

An Island?

SEVENTEENTH-CENTURY English poet John Donne wrote these familiar words: "No man is an island, entire of itself; every man is a piece of the continent, a part of the main."

What do you think he meant?

_____

_____

_____

You are only one individual, but you do have an influence on others. You may have certain talents and gifts in life. And God has called you to be his representative. But he never meant for you to be an island, a lone person witnessing for him separate from others. He has placed you in a very powerful unit of other people—so powerful, in fact, that Jesus said, "All the powers of hell will not conquer it" (Matthew 16:18).

What is this powerful unit you are a part of? What is it called?

_____

The human body has many parts, but the many parts make up only one body. So it is with the body of Christ. Some of us are Jews, some are Gentiles, some are slaves, and some are free. But we have all been baptized into Christ's body by one Spirit, and we have all received the same Spirit. (1 Corinthians 12:12-13)

Your youth group is a local representation of Christ's body, the church. And it is his Body—your CrossCulture army—that is empowered by his Spirit to be a shining light to the world.

I am called personally to fulfill my mission to share Christ's message with others, right? But what does that have to do with the body of Christ? Read this passage and then answer the question below.

> *Just as our bodies have many parts and each has a specific function, so it is with Christ's body. We are parts of his one body, and each of us has different work to do. And since we are all one body in Christ, we belong to each other, and each of us needs all the others. (Romans 12:4-5)*

Based on Romans 12, do you need others in your CrossCulture army to fulfill your mission? Take time to think through your answer. Do you think God wants you to fulfill your mission in concert with others, or is it okay to act alone in your call?

_____

_____

_____

_____

_____

Even Jesus wasn't on his own in his mission. You might think since Christ was God in human form, he could do anything he wanted to do. But Jesus said, "The Son can do nothing by himself. He does only what he sees the Father doing" (John 5:19). He later said, "The words that I say are not my own, but my Father who lives in me does his work through me" (John 14:10).

Since even Jesus himself didn't do anything on his own, but acted in harmony with his Father, do you think we should fulfill our mission as one army?

         ⭕ yes   ⭕ no   ⭕ not sure

What would being a representative of Christ in harmony with your CrossCulture army (Christ's body) look like? What would living your Christian life in harmony with your Christian friends require?

_____

_____

_____

Week Seven
Day 2
Week Seven
Day 2
Week Seven
Day 2
Week Seven
Day 2
Week Seven
Day 2
Week Seven
Day 2
Week Seven
Day 2
Week Seven
Day 2
Week Seven
Day 2
Week Seven
Day 2
Week Seven
Day 2
Week Seven
Day 2
Week Seven

_____

_____

_____

Identify some characteristics of a group that acted as one body—a body that belonged to one another and needed one another. Check (✓) those that apply.

○ Unified
○ Interdependent
○ Boring
○ Attractive
○ Productive
○ Strong
○ Wimpish
○ Multi-talented
○ Leaderless
○ Embarrassed

Here are the words of Jesus:

"I have given them the glory you gave me, so that they may be one, as we are—I in them and you in me, all being perfected into one. Then the world will know that you sent me and will understand that you love them as much as you love me." (John 17:22-23)

"Just as I have loved you, you should love each other. Your love for one another will prove to the world that you are my disciples." (John 13:34-35)

God's design is to win the world by drawing people to him through his body—you and your CrossCulture army. When you are loving God and one another, caring for and meeting each other's needs, you become a magnet—an attractive group that prompts an outside world to say, "I need that."

My Assignment: Think Strategically

BECAUSE YOU are one in Christ and are unified as an army of one, you have the power of one. Christ is head of your local CrossCulture army, and you can count on the fact that he wants you to represent him individually yet together with your group.

What are some ways you as a group can reach out and be a living representative of Christ? Put down any idea that comes to mind.

_____

_____

_____

_____

_____

_____

_____

_____

During your next group session, you'll be given the opportunity to share your ideas, and brainstorm strategic ways to reach out to others as a group.

Special Note

THIS IS THE LAST WEEK of your workbook and daily devotionals with your e-prayer group. Ask your youth leader about continuing to get daily devotionals. You can get a full year (365 days) of devotionals online. Check it out with your group leader.

Also, we need your help. On the last page of this workbook, you will find an evaluation form. Will you fill it out? It will help us know how to create better workbooks in the future. Thanks.

**Access your daily devotionals at www.MyCrossCulture/prayer or come back to this workbook for your daily devotional assignments.

Week Seven
Day 2
Week Seven
Day 2
Week Seven
Day 2
Week Seven
Day 2
Week Seven
Day 2
Week Seven
Day 2
Week Seven
Day 2
Week Seven
Day 2
Week Seven
Day 2
Week Seven
Day 2
Week Seven
Day 2
Week Seven
Day 2
Week Seven
Day 2
Week Seven
Day 2
Week Seven

Days 3–5
Week Seven
Days 3–5
Week Seven
Days 3–5
Week Seven
Days 3–5
Week Seven
Days 3–5
Week Seven
Days 3–5
Week Seven
Days 3–5
Week Seven
Days 3–5
Week Seven
Days 3–5
Week Seven
Days 3–5
Week Seven
Days 3–5
Week Seven
Days 3–5
Week Seven
Days 3–5

Daily Devotional

Week 7 Day 3

Read John 13:34—35

Why does your Christlike love for your Christian friends prove to the world that you belong to Jesus?

_____

_____

_____

_____

Week 7 Day 4

Read Philippians 2:15

What words and actions can you display today to show that Jesus is real?

_____

_____

_____

_____

Week 7 Day 5

Read Matthew 28:19

In what ways would God be pleased to use your CrossCulture army to lead others from death to new life?

_____

_____

_____

_____

Week 8 | Group Session 8

FOR SEVEN WEEKS now, we've been learning about the CrossCulture life, and becoming part of the CrossCulture Revolution.

The CrossCulture Revolution is a worldwide phenomenon, but it is a Culture of One. The last week of his life, Jesus prayed:

"I am praying not only for these disciples but also for all who will ever believe in me because of their testimony. My prayer for all of them is that they will be one, just as you and I are one, Father— that just as you are in me and I am in you, so they will be in us, and the world will believe you sent me." (John 17:20-21)

Think about this: If you are a follower of Jesus Christ and a part of the Cross-Culture Revolution, Jesus was praying for YOU! What was his prayer for you?

That

_____

_____

Has that happened for you? Has Jesus' prayer for you been answered in recent weeks? (circle one)

YES   NO   I DON'T KNOW

These past seven weeks we've discussed four different, crucial aspects of the CrossCulture Life. Do you remember what they are?

I.   A _____ LIFE.

The CrossCulture life is a _____ life that has had a sinful record nailed to Christ's cross and been made alive in him (see Col. 2:13-14).

Those who become Christians become new persons. They are not the same anymore, for the old life is gone. A new life has begun. (2 Corinthians 5:17)

2. A _____ LIFE.

    The CrossCulture life is a _____ life that shoulders a cross of sacrifice daily (see Luke 9:23).

    I have been crucified with Christ. I myself no longer live, but Christ lives in me. (Galatians 2:19-20, NLT)

3. A _____ LIFE.

    The CrossCulture life is a life at _____ _____ with the culture, not conforming to the sinful ways of the world.

    Don't copy the behavior and customs of this world, but let God transform you into a new person. (Romans 12:2)

4. A _____ IN LIFE.

    The CrossCulture life has a _____ to share the Gospel across all cultures.

    God has given us the task of reconciling people to him...We are Christ's ambassadors, and God is using us to speak to you. (2 Corinthians 5:18, 20)

    What three things will I do as Christ's ambassador to play a part in transforming my school and church and community?

1. _____

2. _____

3. _____

    What three things can we do corporately as a group or as a church?

1. _____

2. _____

3. _____

The Revolt Evaluation Form

How old are you? _____   ◯ Male   ◯ Female

1. ◯ I went through this workbook with my youth group.

2. ◯ I went through this workbook by myself, not with my youth group.

3. Did you use the MyCrossCulture e-prayer group site?

   ◯ Yes   ◯ No

4. Did you make a commitment as a result of this course or *The Revolt* video series?

   ◯ First time commitment to Christ   ◯ A recommitment to Christ
   ◯ Neither

5. Tell us how this workbook helped you the most.

   _____

   _____

   _____

   _____

6. Can you give us a suggestion on how to make these kinds of workbooks better?

   _____

   _____

   _____

   _____

Please remove this page, fold in thirds, and mail this form to:
   Josh McDowell Ministry
   P.O. Box 4126
   Copley, OH 44321

135

JOSH McDOWELL MINISTRY

P.O. Box 4126

Copley, OH 44321

Incite A CROSSCULTURE™ Revolution

Here is a foundational family of products to transform a generation into passionate followers of Christ who know why they believe what they believe.

BE CONVINCED OF WHY YOU BELIEVE

Beyond Belief to Convictions Book to Adults

Having Christian convictions means being so thoroughly convinced that Christ and his Word are both objectively true and relationally meaningful that you act on your beliefs regardless of the consequences. *Beyond Belief* contains the blueprint for a revolution in the lives of young people. It will help you lead them to a real encounter with God and transform them into passionate followers of Christ. *Beyond Belief to Convictions* SC: 0-8423-7409-4

The CrossCulture Revolution Book to Adults

Why call for a revolution? Josh and Ron cite at least three compelling reasons: (1) Despite the efforts of the church, Christian schools, and Christian families, the vast majority of our kids lead lives virtually no different from non-Christians; (2) our kids consistently make wrong moral choices; and (3) upon leaving home, our young people do not remain in the church. The authors offer a spiritual revolution manifesto for the church and family to raise up a "cross culture"—a transformed generation of passionate followers of Christ. *The CrossCulture Revolution* 0-8423-7976-2

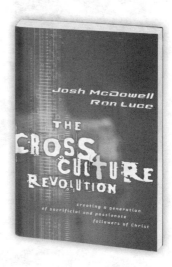

In Search of Certainty Book to Adults

Statistics are alarming. Eighty-eight percent of the U.S. population does not believe in a moral absolute. Postmodernism has undermined the concept of absolute truth in the past generation, leaving even Christians groping for meaning and certainty in their lives. This book exposes the irrationalities of atheistic positions, showing that God is real and truth is absolute, and only trust in him can provide certainty that life has meaning and fulfillment. An excellent book to give to a seeker friend.
In Search of Certainty 0-8423-7972-X

Begin Your CROSSCULTURE™ Revolution at www.BeyondBelief.com

BE CONVINCED OF WHY YOU BELIEVE

Josh McDowell's Youth Devotions 2
Josh McDowell's Family Devotions 2
to Youth/Families

"We are not fighting against people made of flesh and blood, but against the evil rulers and authorities of the unseen world . . ." (Ephesians 6:12, NLT). More than ever our young people need a spiritual defense. This second installment of Josh's best-selling youth and family devotions offer 365 daily devotional encounters with the true Power Source to strengthen your family spiritually and provide your young people with a resource that will help them combat today's culture.

Josh McDowell's Youth Devotions 2 0-8423-4096-3
Josh McDowell's Family Devotions 2 0-8423-5625-8

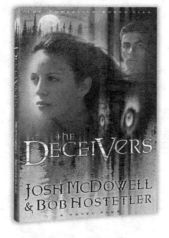

The Deceivers Book to Youth

Written in the popular NovelPlus format, this book combines the adventures of Sarah Milford and Ryan Ortiz and their search for meaning, along with Josh's insights found in sections called "The Inside Story."

In dramatic fashion *The Deceivers* explains that unless Christ is who he claims to be—the true Son of God—then his offer to redeem us and provide meaning to life can't be real. This book presents not only the compelling evidence for the deity of Christ but also how God's plan is to transform us into a new creature with an intimate relationship with him. *The Deceivers* 0-8423-7969-X

Children Demand a Verdict Book to Children

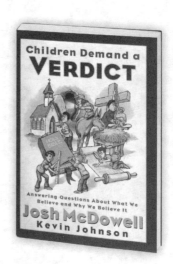

Children need clear and direct answers to their questions about God, the Bible, sin, death, etc. Directed to children ages 7–11, this question-and-answer book tackles 77 tough issues with clarity and relevance, questions such as: Why did God make people? How do we know Jesus was God? How could God write a book? Is the Bible always right? Are parts of the Bible make-believe? Why did Jesus die? Did Jesus really come back to life? Does God always forgive me? Why do people die? Will I come back to life like Jesus?

Children Demand a Verdict 0-8423-7971-1

BE COMMITTED TO WHAT YOU BELIEVE

Video Series for Adult Groups

This 5-part interactive video series features Josh McDowell sharing how your young people have adopted distorted beliefs about God, truth, and reality and what you as adults can do about it. Step by step he explains how to lead your kids to know "why we believe what we believe" and how that is truly relevant to their everyday lives. This series provides the perfect launch for your group to build the true foundation of Christianity in the lives of the family, beginning with adults.

The series includes 5 video sessions of approximately 25 minutes each, a comprehensive Leader's Guide with reproducible handouts, the *Beyond Belief to Convictions* book, and a complimentary copy of *The Deceivers* NovelPlus book. (Also available on DVD.)

Belief Matters Video Series 0-8423-8018-3

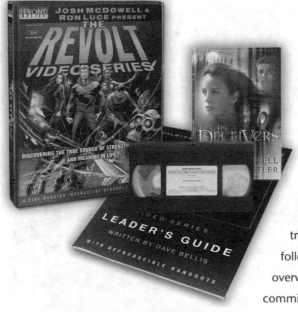

Video Series for Youth Groups

Combining a powerful message, compelling video illustrations, and captivating group activities, this series will enable you to lead your students to this convincing conclusion: the ways of the world do not produce true meaning in life—only Christ as the true Son of God can transform our "dead lives" into a dynamic and meaningful life in relationship with him. Josh and Ron have created this interactive series to incite a revolution—a revolution to transform your young people into a generation of sacrificial and passionate followers of Christ. As a foundational building block of Christianity this series offers overwhelming evidence that Christ is the Messiah and challenges each student to commit totally to him.

The series includes 5 dramatic video illustrations, Leader's Guide of teaching lessons with reproducible handouts for group activities, and *The Deceivers* NovelPlus book. (Also available on DVD.) ***The Revolt Video Series*** 0-8423-8016-7

BE CHANGED BY WHO YOU BELIEVE

Workbook for Adult Groups

Combining interactive group discussion with daily activities, this workbook helps you overcome the distorted views of Christ and biblical truth held by most children and youth today. It will help you lead them to a fresh encounter with the "God who is passionate about his relationship with you" (Exodus 34:14, NLT). The daily activities reveal a credible, real, and relevant Christ you can share with each family member.

The workbook study provides 8 solid group teaching sessions for the weekly at-home assignments to model the message before others.

Belief Matters Workbook Wkbk: 0-8423-8010-8 Ld. Gd: 0-8423-8011-6

Workbook for Youth Groups

When your students reject the world's counterfeit way of life, what will life in Christ really be like for them? This 8-session course helps each of your students realize that new life in Christ is about transformation, about belonging to Christ and one another in his Body, about knowing who they really are, and about living out their mission in life.

The Revolt Workbook is an 8-session youth group interactive course followed up with students engaging in two daily exercises per week. This study is the perfect follow-up to the companion *Revolt Video Series*. *The Revolt Workbook* Wkbk: 0-8423-7978-9 Ld. Gd: 0-8423-7979-7

Workbook for Children's Groups

To raise up the next generation of committed followers of Christ, we must start when they are young. These workbooks for children grades 1–3 and grades 4–6 present the foundational truth of why Christ came to earth. Written in simple terms, they lead your children to realize why doing wrong has separated them from God and why only Christ can bring them into a close family relationship with God.

In 8 fun-filled sessions, your children will learn why Christ is the true way and all other ways are false. These sessions lead children to a loving encounter with the "God who is passionate about his relationship with [them]" (Exodus 34:14, NLT).

True or False Workbook Younger Wkbk: 0-8423-8012-4 Older Wkbk: 0-8423-8013-2 Ld. Gd: 0-8423-8014-0

**Contact your Christian Supplier to obtain these resources
and begin the revolution in your home, church, and community.**

Life-changing Events & Training

MINISTRY EVENTS FOR ALL AGES

Minister/Leader Banquet
Adult/Parent Seminar
High School Assembly
Acquire The Fire & Josh McDowell Youth Event

These events are designed to inspire, motivate, and challenge you, your adult congregation, and your young people. Take advantage of each of these four events in your city to incite or perpetuate your own CrossCulture revolution within your church and youth group. Josh McDowell and Ron Luce are locking arms together in these ministry events to partner with you on the local level. Thirty-two cities will host these events to act as a catalyst for spiritual revolution.

For more information log on to www.beyondbelief.com and go to the "Events" section.

CROSSCULTURE YOUTH MINISTRY TRAINING

To truly see a revolution in youth culture, a revolution in youth ministry must take place. We have all tried the tricks, but most youth are still looking to pop culture as a model for their lifestyle. Youth ministry as we know it is not cutting it. Together we must unite to develop a message and resources to truly combat a postmodern culture. This is war and we need tools to spark a revolution.

CrossCulture Youth Ministry Summit is a youth ministry seminar conducted each fall. It is presented through a partnership of respected youth ministries committed

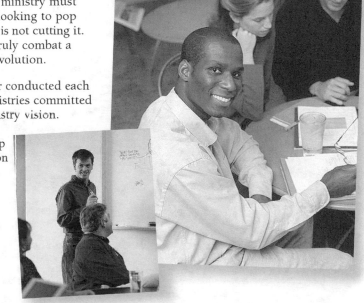

to helping you reach your ministry vision. You will be ministered to by world-class speakers, fellowship with men and women of passion

CROSSCULTURE™

and vision, and leave fully equipped to revolutionize your youth ministry and community. Use this annual event as a time to be challenged and equipped to perpetuate a spiritual revolution.

For more information log on to www.beyondbelief.com and go to the "Training" section.

Begin your CrossCulture Revolution at www.beyondbelief.com